BREAKING THROUGH

BREAKING

Beating the Odds Shot after Shot

THROUGH

CHAMIQUE
HOLDSCLAW

Breaking Through: *Beating the Odds Shot After Shot*

ISBN: 978-0-9850298-0-7
ePub ISBN: 978-0-9850298-1-4
Mobi ISBN: 978-0-9850298-2-1

Library of Congress Control Number: 2012900597

Photography by Desmond.
Cover Design and Interior Layout: AuthorSupport.com

Dedication

I dedicate this book to my
Grandmother June Holdsclaw,
My Mother Bonita Clark,
and Coach Pat Summitt.
You have all given me strength

Visit my website:www.chamiqueholdsclaw.com
Follow me on twitter: @chold1

TABLE OF CONTENTS

TABLE OF CONTENTS (contiuned)

Foreword by Pat Summitt

Every coach, no matter what sport you coach, hopes one day they will have an opportunity to come across "a once in a lifetime player." A player who is so phenomenally gifted they wear the sport like their own skin. They are totally one with what they do.

Back in the 1990's, there was talk of such a player in the women's basketball game from New York City. She was described as fluid, fearless, streetwise but with a calm gentleness. She was labeled a once in a lifetime player – a franchise.

She was Chamique Holdsclaw.

The first time I saw her play, the game of basketball seemed effortless to her. The ball was like an extension of her hand. I wouldn't call her game flashy. She was so fluid that you didn't realize how many points she had scored or rebounds she had taken off the glass until the final box score.

Initially, I found it interesting that a player with such a big game would have such a quiet "old soul" demeanor. That was, until I met her grandmother and guardian, June Holdsclaw.

June Holdsclaw was Chamique's heart and soul. Instantly, June and I made a connection and I had a great rapport with her from our first meeting. I think Chamique sensed that grandmother approved of my disciplined ways, my commitment at the University of Tennessee to graduating our players and preparing them for life after basketball.

Grandmother June provided Chamique with a safe haven in Astoria Queens when her tumultuous adolescent world tipped over at the age of 12. Even better, life in Astoria Queens brought the game of basketball into Chamique's world. Mique even called it her "first love."

When Chamique arrived at the University of Tennessee in the fall of 1995, she was immediately embraced by her teammates. She quickly connected with fellow freshman and point guard Kellie Jolly from Sparta, Tennessee. They hit it off and nicknamed each other "city" and "country."

I knew from day one there was something special about Chamique and it had nothing to do with basketball. She was genuine. She was persistent and stubborn. She was driven to achieve in all aspects of her life and she didn't make excuses. I liked that in her.

I'm sure she thought I had lost my mind when I threw her out of practice one day. I told her she wasn't working hard and she rolled her eyes at me. That's it, I tossed her. After practice I called June and told her to expect a call from Chamique. She probably wanted to transfer. I explained what had happened and June told me she was behind me 100 percent.

Chamique and I sat down and talked about it the next day. Looking back, I think she and I may have developed the best communication bond of any of the players I have ever coached.

Along the way as a Lady Vol, Chamique received her degree on time. She was a four-time Kodak All-American, Player of the Year, the Sullivan Award winner, Southeastern Conference Most Valuable Player and MVP of the Final Four. She helped to carry three consecutive NCAA title banners back to the Knoxville campus in 1996, 1997 and 1998. The City of Knoxville even named a street near Thompson-Boling Arena in her honor when she graduated in 1999.

We were all so excited for Chamique when she was selected as the top pick of the 1999 WNBA draft by the Washington Mystics. I know June was thrilled to have her closer to home. June was so proud of the young woman Chamique had blossomed into during her four years at Tennessee. Mique was the first to say she owed her success to her grandmother's determined spirit.

June died of a heart attack on May 27, 2002. An inconsolable Chamique asked me to speak at the funeral. For someone I thought I knew so well, Chamique managed to hide behind a mask after June passed away so suddenly. For the next couple of years, she threw herself into basketball and had some of her best years as a pro. Little did I know she was putting on a brave face on the outside but her soul was totally grief stricken and severe depression hid just behind her easy smile.

I realize now, without her grandmother, Chamique had lost the true north setting in her life. When she opened up to me about her clinical depression, she had already been down the path for a long time.

It took a great deal of courage for Chamique to share some of the most difficult and challenging moments in her life in *Breaking Through – Beating the Odds Shot after Shot.* I realized after reading her amazingly open and candid story that Chamique's life journey exemplifies what the great astronomer Galileo said centuries ago:

> *"We cannot teach people anything; we can only help them discover it within themselves."*

Pat Summitt

Introduction

I looked up at the ceiling of the ambulance, confused. I soon realized that I was being rushed to Centinela Hospital in Los Angeles. As we tore down the street, the sounds of flowing oxygen and machines controlling my heart filled the air. The EMTs hovered above my body, taking my blood pressure and doing their best to keep me alive. I went in and out of consciousness, wondering how I'd let it get this far. I was taught to be stronger than this and yet, here I was, possibly minutes away from death.

I was so tired of always having to be the strong one. My grandmother was gone now, and I wanted nothing more than to be with her. In the days leading up to this, my thoughts had been filled with images of me losing control of my car or jumping from a building to end it all. I didn't see a way out of the darkness that had come to consume me, so I finally chose to overdose on my anti-depression medication. The self I once knew was fractured and I just could not fit the pieces back together.

During my stay at the hospital, I suffered through one of the worst nights of my life. I had severe hallucinations; I was freezing cold, and vomited on a good friend. I repeatedly asked my friend and the doctors if I was going to die. The next day as they moved me to another room and under suicide watch, the doctor came to me and told me how lucky I'd been. He said I could have really messed myself up, aside from actually dying. That's when I promised myself (and God) that I would never let it get this bad again.

A few years later I finally I came clean to the public about my personal struggle with depression and my attempted suicide. When I told Kelli Anderson from *Sports Illustrated* my story, a weight was lifted off of my shoulders. I opened my life up to others and they helped heal me by connecting with me and letting me know I wasn't alone. I have since received hundreds of letters and messages from people telling me how my strength—that same strength I resented and doubted—was their inspiration. To prevent anyone from having the horrible experience that I did, I started traveling around the U.S.A speaking with different groups about my mental health issues. I've since come a long way from being a shy person who didn't understand the power of her voice to a woman who feels comfortable connecting with thousands and advocating for mental health.

Depression is a disease like any other, and awareness needs to be raised so that we can more easily talk about this very personal issue. I'm trying to do my part to help eliminate the stigma and take away the shame that is associated with this disease by talking openly about it, and by writing this book. I wrote this book to let people know that "Tough times don't last but tough people do"—thanks Coach Summitt, for planting that seed in my head during my days in college.

I hope you all benefit from my words and my story.

FIRST
QUARTER

CHAPTER 1

Inside the Walls

I was born Chamique Shaunta Holdsclaw, on August 9th 1977 to Willie Johnson and Bonita Holdsclaw. My parents were young and in love; my mom only 17 and my dad 20. They met in the Astoria housing projects behind my grandmother's building in Queens, New York. My mother was sitting outside with a group of her friends when my father first approached her. The conversation was casual but my father's quiet and confident demeanor soon won her over. He was a compliment to my mother's more headstrong and feisty personality. They quickly fell in love, and New York City was the backdrop to their romantic playground.

After two years of dating, my mom found out that she was pregnant. My mother had high hopes of what she thought life would be like as a mother and a wife. In reality, however, it was difficult for a pregnant high school senior. She wanted to drop out of school, but she was forbidden to do so by my grandmother. Instead, she continued through her last year, with me growing inside of her. The day she graduated from Van Buren High School, she walked down the aisle and received two diplomas, one for herself and one for me. My dad was so proud that my mom had graduated and was excited that he was going to be a father. He wanted to do whatever he could to create a stable environment for his growing family. Two months after my mother's graduation, I came into the world.

After I was born, we left the hospital and went to my grandmother's,

June Holdsclaw's house. That was where my grandmother showed my parents how to take care of me, a newborn. She patiently molded and guided them into being better parents. She was always an arm's length away for us. Luckily for my parents, I took on my dad's easygoing personality. I didn't even need a pacifier. I was my parents' perfect little miracle and they were sublimely happy.

Throughout this process, a special bond was forged between my father and my grandmother. He was raised in Mullins, South Carolina, and came to New York after high school to work on his relationship with his estranged mother. My father's parents had never married and his mother had moved to New York when he was younger. He had decided to stay with his grandmother to finish up school in the south and to be with his father. My grandmother June was a nurturer to all and my father was no exception.

Three years after I was born, our family once again expanded with the birth of my brother, Davon Adrien Holdsclaw. I remember it like it was yesterday. My mom and I were home on Sutphin Boulevard in Jamaica, Queens watching "The Odd Couple" when she suddenly started screaming with labor pains. She told me to call my father, who was away working as a mechanic. I so vividly remember passing her the phone and her yelling for him to come home. Confused and scared, I waited for my father to walk through the door and save the day. I can remember saying, "Mom it will be okay, don't cry," in an attempt to soothe her pain. (Yes, even as a three-year-old my heart was big.) What seemed like hours later, my dad came through the door playing his usual part of the hero. He packed my mother and me into the back of his green Monte Carlo and sped us to the hospital.

The first face I saw when we pulled up to Booth Memorial Hospital was Grandma June. I ran to her and jumped into her arms. She was the calm among the commotion. She walked me through the hallways as we waited for the arrival of my brother. We passed by the nursery and I can remember asking over and over if each baby was my brother. I was excited to be a big sister because I was finally going to have someone to play with. What I didn't know was that my brother was born prematurely, and that he would suffer in life because of my mom's poor decisions while she was carrying him.

There was no shortage of love during my early childhood years. Each day I anticipated my dad's return home from work. I appreciated my grandmother June telling me how much she loved me. I loved running around my Aunt Ruby's house picking up quarters—for some reason, she believed in throwing all of her change on the floor. We took trips to the park and I always had new and fun toys.

But I would soon learn that nothing was perfect. Like most children, I was blinded by toys and hugs. What I didn't see was the stupors my parents drank themselves into over the weekends and on holidays. Soon the laughter turned into arguments and confrontations. The more they drank, the louder things got. Doors slammed, objects were thrown, and the love I'd once felt began to diminish. The more empty beer cans that piled up next to the kitchen sink, the more aggressive the language between my parents became. The smell of alcohol replaced the delicious aroma of home-cooked meals.

One time while drunk and returning from my aunt's house in the Bronx, my father drove us over the Triborough Bridge and lost control. Our car spun around three times and ended up hitting the side rail. Once the car had come to a stop and my father realized all was relatively well, he nonchalantly got behind the wheel and took us back home.

As I grew older the drinking got worse. The fog of childhood began to clear and I could soon see what my parents had become. At just six years of age, I wanted to protect my brother from the horrors that I had seen. I wanted him to remain in the fog. I wanted to be his shelter from the chaos that was now our home. He became my shadow and I didn't feel comfortable unless I was with him. I was his protector.

I vividly remember one time when, after another night of partying, my parents began to once again argue. The back-and-forth insults between them grew louder and more offensive. My father stormed out and my mother proceeded to blast Al Green so loud that the walls shook. She played the same song over and over, and through all of this I tried to comfort my brother as he lay in the bed in my arms. I did my best to assure him that everything would be okay. The next morning my father returned home as though nothing had happened, and we were a family again.

For my brother I was a great pretender, acting as if our closets weren't full of dark secrets. I had to be strong. There were times when my mother would drink and push me around to make me cry. She would tell me how bad of a father my dad was. My mother knew precisely what to say to hurt me. My father and I were close; no matter how bad it got within our home, he did his best to be a present father. He wasn't as heavy of a drinker as my mother was. He somehow never let the alcohol control him or impact the work ethic that drove him to provide for his family.

In the increasingly rare moments when my parents were not drinking, I recalled glimpses of the happiness I used to know. They made it a point to praise me for the work I did in school. From kindergarten to the fifth grade I was in honor classes and focused on my schoolwork. It was a distraction that I gladly welcomed. School was a way to garner the attention I'd once received from my parents before their abuse began, and even after their drinking, my mom made it a point to be on top of the neatness of my work. She would have me do the work over and over until it met her standards. It was a chore, but I was happy at the attention I received from her.

Outside of the walls of my house I was quiet, tall and awkward. I did my best to blend into the background. I was shy and often felt embarrassed by the antics of my parents. I was the polar opposite of my mother; I did not want to be noticed. My first grade teacher, Mrs. Turner, was the first to see beyond my shyness. I was her favorite, and this did not sit well with another girl in my class. One day, while playing Duck-Duck-Goose, in a jealous rage the other girl scratched my face as she ran by. I stood up to defend myself but stopped dead in my tracks at the thought of how my mother would react. That afternoon when I stepped off the bus, my mom immediately noticed the scratch across my face. She asked, "What happened?" and I told her. She then asked, "What did you do after it happened?" and I replied, "Nothing." She then told me, "If you don't whoop her butt right now, I am going to whoop yours when we get home." And that was the day I learned how to fight. I walked up to the other girl and pushed her down. I then started to kick her. I felt like I had no choice, and I feared getting a spanking for not standing up for myself.

Around this time, at age six, I started developing a strong dislike for my mom's drunken escapades, and so I spent as much time out of the house as I could, along with my little shadow of a brother. I befriended some of the kids from our building and we would run up and down the hallways playing. My best friend in the building was Nicole Howell and she became my safe haven. She and her mom lived five floors down from us. Her mom, Ms. Sharon, would take us different places throughout the city. One day, Nicole asked me why my mom drank so much. I was so embarrassed when I realized that everyone knew our secrets. Yet, it didn't matter to Nicole. We were friends and had fun together. We had our little crew of about ten other kids who also lived in the building. We would jump on soiled mattresses plied up at the curbs and we'd ride the subway all over New York City. We did things that no responsible adult would ever let their kids do alone; at least not nowadays.

In New York during the 80s you could use a paper clip and connect with the receiver on public pay phones, allowing us to make free phone calls. So we would prank call people for hours. I don't think I ever laughed so hard, nor had such fun. The streets were all I knew. We loved to hang out at the Queens Borough Public library or people-watch on Jamaica Avenue. When I was outside of my home I could just be a kid. No drinking, no screaming, just me and my friends having a good time.

While I grew outside of my house, the trouble inside grew as well. When it came time to come home at the end of the day, there were countless times where my brother and I were left stranded outside. We would bang on the door to get in for what seemed like hours. Our parents would be passed out drunk inside, unable to hear our knocks. On those nights we would find ourselves at Nicole's house. Most of our neighbors knew what was going on and did their best to look after my brother and me, but everyone has their boiling point. I had little idea my neighbors would be the catalyst that would change my life.

One night, like so many times before, my mom had gone out with friends and left us with my father. The night started as any other. My dad was cooking us dinner, and I still remember the meal: collard greens and pepper steak. My brother and I asked if we could go play at Nicole's house until dinner was ready. He told us we could, but to be back in an hour. After the hour had passed we returned to find a locked door and no answer. We could smell the aroma of food cooking and hear the music playing through the door, so we knew he was still there. We knocked and knocked and knocked until the police were eventually called. When they arrived, they somehow got the door open only to find my dad passed out drunk inside. The music was blasting and the food was beginning to burn.

I was 11 years old, and my brother was just 8; we were confused and scared. That night the police drove us down to the precinct, where we were met by a social worker. She did her best to comfort us and reassure us that we would both be safe. She then allowed me to call our grandmother, who came as quickly as she could. The situation was explained and we would be allowed to go home with her. I was terrified. Things had never been this bad. Moments after my grandmother's arrival, in stormed my mother, intoxicated. A neighbor had told her what had happened. She pleaded with them to let us return home, but it was clear she wasn't fit to parent us. They gave my grandmother temporary custody until a caseworker could make a visit to our home. But this was only the beginning of the storm.

I didn't want us to end up in foster care and was concerned that they wouldn't let us live with my grandmother. Social workers conducted interviews with us, carefully looking over our living situation. They wanted to find out if we would be happy with my grandmother and if any sort of abuse had been going on in our home. I recall them specifically asking about how I would feel attending a new school and how I felt towards my grandmother. After all the questions, it was then decided that the best place for us was to remain with our grandmother in her home. The state had decided my mother would need to complete rehab before she would be able to regain custody. My father, on the other hand, did not have to meet any requirements. This was because my parents were not married. My father's name was not even stated on my birth certificate.

My world turned inside out. It was the middle of the school year and I was being moved to a new school and new home. My grandmother still lived in the Astoria housing projects. I was shaken, but remained hopeful that things would turn out for the better. I tried my best to see this as an adventure. I was comforted to see kids running around the neighborhood when we arrived. Maybe I could be happy here after all? Across from my grandmother's building sat another building, and in between was a large grass field where kids would play tag, football and other sports. To the left of her building were the basketball courts. The projects had a low hum of constant movement. I was a fish out of the water with no friends, searching for a place to belong.

My Aunt Anita, my mother's sister, would help me to find that place. Although she didn't live there, she worked the summer program in the neighborhood. Aunt Anita had a close friend named Ms. Donella, who happened to have a son a little younger than I, named Andrew. I wasn't into jumping rope, or playing with dolls or makeup, so I fit right in with him and the other boys. We would play all sorts of sports, but Andrew particularly liked to play basketball. I would go with him to shoot every chance I got. My life at my grandmother's home was starting to feel somewhat normal. Too bad the same can't be said for school. When my grandmother had taken me down to I.S.126 in order to enroll, I remember how nervous and scared I was as the other kids glared at me. I was the new kid on the block and my only saving grace was that some of the girls in my class also lived in my building, so I was able to make friends with them. My cousin Kewan also went to the same school. Having him there gave me a sense of security and comfort. I knew that as long as he was there, no one would give me a hard time.

We eventually fell into a comfortable routine. Each day I knew what to expect, unlike when we lived with my parents. Every day I would walk to school with the girls from my building and after school I would pick my brother up on the way home. We would then go to our sitter, Miss Jeanie's house, until my grandmother got home from work. When we arrived home, each day we would do our homework and then head outside to play. I would head straight for the courts with Andrew and the other guys. For the first time in a long while, I could see growth in myself.

Life in the projects seemed to be just what my brother and I needed. But like most kids growing up there, one rarely gets through their childhood unscathed. I hadn't been there even two months before the teasing started. The girls that I walked to school with and thought were my friends had turned on me. I was called a "flat leaver" which meant that as soon as I had the chance, I would ditch them and go play with the boys. I was also called a "tomboy" because I didn't want to play Double Dutch or do those girly types of things.

These confrontations soon carried over to school. One day, a girl who was known for being a fighter confronted me. She was strong and aggressive but I was tall and athletic, so I was confident about my chances of surviving. She and her friends circled around me in one of the staircases and said it was time to fight. She pushed me, and I pushed back. After minutes of tussling, I somehow had her head in my hands and was kneeing her in the face. I have to say it was not my proudest moment, but I had to defend myself. After that day, I was left alone and no longer teased. Thankfully, my grandmother never found out about that little incident, since no teachers had seen what had happened.

Each day with my grandmother was truly a blessing. She gave us a clear definition of the word "normal." We ate dinner as a family and talked about our days. There was no more running around aimlessly. For the first time since I was a small child I had direction. My grandmother offered us stability and structure. But it was a struggle to give up my freedoms at first. I could no longer enjoy subway trips or gallivanting through the city. Instead my brother and I found ourselves at the Boys and Girls Club and attending church on Sundays. I would try my best to get out of going to church, but my grandmother quickly found a way to remedy that: if I didn't go to church, I would not be allowed to go out and play basketball afterward. Sunday was a big day on the courts and I didn't want to miss out. One Sunday I opted out of church knowing that I ran the risk of not being allowed to go and play. Like I knew she would, my grandmother told me not to leave our apartment. I waited until she left for church and proceeded to do the opposite of what she had asked. I knew I had at least two hours of uninterrupted hoop time. We are Lutheran, and services were usually about that long, plus she would sit and chat with her friends once church was over. So I called my friends and we headed down to the courts. I was enjoying my rebellious Sunday hoop-fest when, in what seemed like slow motion, my grandmother walked past the courts. Our eyes locked and she said nothing as she continued on to our building. Just like any kid would, I continued to play. Boy was that the wrong move! Moments later she returned to the courts belt in hand yelling at me to get upstairs. Needless to say, I didn't see the courts for a while. I was the laughingstock of the courts, but I had brought it upon myself. The guys didn't let me live that one down for a while.

Although I was now in a safer and overall better environment than before, I still missed my parents. However dysfunctional the situation, they were my parents and I loved them. I had grown accustomed to doing what I needed in order to survive when I was with them. I used to steal money from my mom's purse when she was drinking so that I could buy food for my brother and me. It was still foreign for me not to have to worry about being sent to the store to buy alcohol for my mom. Her favorite was pink champagne. The guy behind the register would always ask me why my mother drank so much, but maybe what he should have done was refused to sell it to me. I would just bury my head with shame. Though those things were all behind me, I couldn't help but think about them from time to time.

While we were staying with my grandmother my mother was at Smithers, a facility that would help her deal with her addiction to alcohol. I always felt strange and uncomfortable each time we would visit her there. It was new for me to see her no longer under the influence. I didn't know the person she was without the alcohol. I would politely smile and listen to her and my grandmother talk about her rehabilitation. We would often walk around the facility meeting her friends, trying to gain a better understanding of what she was going through. During this time my dad's drinking had slowed, too, and he would come visit us several times a week. He never wanted us to feel abandoned or unloved by him. It was hard for him to be away from us. It was the last thing he had ever wanted for his family. He would always assure us that this was temporary and that one day we would be back together as a family.

My surroundings had improved, but no one knew the struggles I was having internally. I had all of these feelings and I didn't know what to do with them. I put on a brave face and tried to be the best big sister, daughter and granddaughter I could be, but it was all too much. I was in 6th grade, eleven years old, and my grades had begun to drop. I started cutting class with some of the other kids in the neighborhood. My rebelliousness was a way for me to take back the control I had lost. I felt dark inside and everything reflected that, even my clothes. At one point, I had missed school for three weeks straight. Once again I was hanging out at the park and taking the train around the city. My friends and I even thought about selling drugs to fund our daily trips.

One day, I skipped school alone. It was freezing outside and I was sitting in the park near the Ravenswood housing projects when a maintenance man approached me. He asked me to follow him into the building where he had worked. I agreed and followed him in. He then asked if I wanted something to eat. Thinking of the ache in my stomach I quickly said yes. We hopped in his car and went to get some food and pastries from a local Greek restaurant. After that we headed back to the park to eat. He then asked if I had a girlfriend. I was very confused, but quickly answered no. Then it clicked in my head: he thought I was a boy. I was dressed in a sweatshirt and pants, a large Triple F.A.T. goose down jacket, and a hat with my hood on. His questions continued. He asked if I'd ever had thoughts about men touching me and if I wanted to touch him. I grew more and more uncomfortable with each question. Finally, I snatched the hood from my head and screamed that I was a girl. Shocked, he apologized. It was about time to pick up my brother from school so I hurried from the bench to my brother's school. Once I arrived to pick him up they had told me that he'd felt sick and gone home early. I assumed our sitter had come and got him and continued on my way home. I casually walked through the projects as I always did. I turned the knob and opened the door to find my grandmother sitting there, furious at me. It turned out that she had stopped by my school earlier that day to tell me I didn't have to pick my brother up from school and found out that I had been delinquent for the past three weeks. I saw an anger in her face that I had never seen before. She was livid at the school and me. She never received a call from the school about me not being there. I had gravely disappointed my grandmother and felt terrible about it. I was ready for whatever punishment I would be given. I was ready for whatever would come my way, but it never came.

Instead I found myself at Alateen, talking to a therapist. Through Alateen I learned how to cope with the stresses of being the child of someone who drinks. When I first started going I hated it and I certainly did not want to share my feelings with strangers. I didn't want to talk about the things that I had considered private. How could they understand or help me? My grandmother insisted that I give it a chance and she kept sending me. I trusted her and her judgment, so I let down my guard and accepted the help I really needed. The change was gradual, but I could see the difference in myself. This process helped my grandmother and I to grow closer. She now realized I wasn't the type of child that needed to be yelled at or spanked in order to get a point across, but that she simply had to talk to me instead.

I refocused on my family and my schooling. But it was too late: near the end of the school year I found out that because of all the days I'd missed, I would be held back. I could blame no one but myself. It was then that my grandmother decided that the New York public school system was not the place for me, that we had failed each other.

CHAPTER 2

My First Love

My grandmother enrolled me into Queens Lutheran School, our church's school. I was given a placement exam to ensure that I could keep up with the workload. I scored well and was placed with my peers in the seventh grade for the next school year. My grandmother and I exhaled deep sighs of relief. It seemed like the worst was behind everyone. The summer was approaching, my mom was getting ready to be released from treatment, and I was back on track.

We were all excited the day my mom was to be released from her program. We met up with her as she said her goodbyes and made her vows to try and remain sober. I was proud of her, but I watched her every move that day. I guess I watched a little too closely and I overheard her say to another patient that she could not wait to be out so that she could get a nice cold beer. I was shocked and crushed. It was even worse to hear the woman reply, "I know what you mean." On that day I realized I might not ever live with my mother again. Thankfully, I was now better equipped to deal with these kinds of disappointments. I was able to look on the bright side. I finally had stability with my grandmother. My new safe haven was Astoria, Queens and I was okay with that.

Soon after my mother's release, we were visited by a social worker. The state decided that we could go back to live with my mother if that was what we wanted. My mother felt that she was ready to be the parent she knew we deserved. I was skeptical and cautious, but decided that I would take the chance and try to live with her once again. My father would not be living with us because he now had his own apartment. It was up to us to make the choice of whether to go or not, and we voted yes.

It wasn't even a month after her release from treatment when I saw her take a drink. I immediately began to scream and cry. She had broken her promise. I was back on the roller coaster once again, and I knew I needed to get off. On the train ride back to my grandmother's I promised myself I would never let my mother hurt me again.

Still, I was determined to enjoy my summer. I was not going to let the disappointment of my mother spoil my fun. I wanted to take advantage of every free day. I played every sport I could, but basketball was my favorite. I had a natural ability and loved the creativity of it. While playing one day I was approached by a man named Reggie. He had apparently seen me playing all summer long with the boys. He was a coach and put me on my first basketball team. I was the only girl on a team full of boys, but I still shined as the best player. Andrew, my next-door neighbor Anthony, and I would wake up early most days and head to Astoria Park. We would hoop and drink twenty-five cent juice. There were times when we would be out literally all day long.

If we weren't on the courts we were off having other adventures. We weren't angels, but we weren't knuckleheads either. Our project was on the East River, which was part of an industrial area, and made up of old factories in the back. That summer we heard of a warehouse fire that had burned down a factory that made toys. Being the curious kids that we were, we decided to see if any of those toys had been left behind. To get there we scaled a gate and trekked along the river over the rocks during low tide. Once we arrived at the factory we saw that someone had beat us there; the gate had been already cut open. We crawled through the gate and over the rocks to the factory. To our surprise, there were toy soldiers and miniature cars. We filled our backpacks up with as many as we could fit. Thrilled at what we had found, we continued on to see what other treasures we could find. Before we could find more toys we heard the murmuring of voices in the distance and took off running. It was a security guard and his dog and I don't think I have ever run as fast as I did that day. We went back through the hole, hopped back over the rocks and once again traversed the river. I was so scared and full of adrenaline that I didn't even notice I had snagged my leg on some barbed wire until I got back to my house. My leg bled for what seemed like an eternity. It eventually stopped, but I would be left with an ugly scar that I still have to this day.

With the summer winding down, I began to think about things from a new perspective. This was when I first realized that the basketball court was my escape. It became my therapist. When I was out there playing it took me to another place. I buried myself in what would become my first love. It gave me great clarity, and as a result I had a new appreciation for everything in my life, especially for my grandmother. We could have been "in the system" and in foster care if she hadn't helped us. She never let me down and I wanted to do the same for her. As I came to know these things and build myself up, though, my mother was once again breaking herself down. By the summer's end she had hit rock bottom once again.

My mother desperately wanted to be a mother to my brother and me, but her desire for alcohol was far greater. I hated alcohol and what it had done to my family. The long hugs and piggyback rides had all disappeared. Alcohol had turned those things into late night visits, crazy outbursts and empty promises. The quality time I used to want with her and my father no longer sounded appealing. My mother would show up at my grandmother's house drunk and angry. She would cuss my grandmother out, and somehow my grandmother would sit there patiently and just take it. In typical June Holdsclaw fashion, she turned the other cheek and focused solely on the love she had for her daughter. No matter how bad the outburst, she would never turn her back on her child. In those moments she would just ask me to pray for my mother. She wanted me to understand that my mother had a disease and that she would need a lot of help to beat it. This was hard for me to accept, especially because of how my brother reacted to the situation. He was a "mama's boy" and wanted nothing more than to be with her. He would cry for her, hoping in his heart that she would be alright. He would faithfully wait for her to come and visit, and even after hours of waiting he would still believe that she would come. I on the other hand, knew better. She had broken my heart one too many times and I had learned to protect myself from her. I was tired of this cycle with my parents and ready for a new chapter of life to begin.

I had mixed feelings as I thought about the approaching school year. Once again, I was starting over. My only comfort was the excitement my grandmother felt about sending me to Queens Lutheran and that we would have orientation before the school year started. It would give me a peek into what I could expect, and surprisingly, I felt confident as I walked for the first time through those halls. Everyone knew and spoke highly of my grandmother, making my adjustment easier. She had a spirit that everyone was attracted to. She drew people into her warmth.

I would soon be challenged academically, but what I looked forward to most was the chance to play for the school's basketball team. This would be the first time I would be playing with other girls and I wondered how I would stack up. Would it be as fun? Would we win any games? Would they talk trash like the guys did? I couldn't wait to find out.

As I expected, I started the school year off with a different energy. I finally felt completely adjusted. I had the support and encouragement I longed for. I felt like I could accomplish anything. Queens Lutheran was so much different than public school. They were significantly more structured. I was challenged to be more disciplined as a person and as a student. My teachers held me accountable for the work I was to do and they taught me responsibility. I respected them.

It was a bit overwhelming at first. I found myself tempted to revert back to my old ways of skipping class and going on joy rides, but this time the school would call as soon as I wasn't accounted for in the classroom. Not knowing this, once I thought I would try my luck and cut school.

That day I enjoyed my usual romp through the city. I went home during the afternoon just like I would have if I had been in school. Over dinner that night we talked about our day as we had every other night together. My grandmother asked me about my day at school and what I learned. Thinking I had gotten away with the day's escapades, I looked my grandmother in her eyes and lied. I told her about my day at school as she listened from across the table. After I was done telling her about my imaginary day, she looked up from her plate and told me that she knew the truth. I remorsefully sat there as she talked to me. She told me she just wanted the best for me, but that I also had to want it for myself. If I was ever going to make it in life I was going to have to change. She then reached across the table and hugged me.

After dinner I went to my room and thought about the things she had said. She was a woman of amazing faith. She raised her children well, sent them through school and provided for them. Now here she was, raising a twelve-year old girl and a nine-year old boy. She was supposed to be getting ready to enjoy retirement after working as Chief of Medical Records at Elmhurst Hospital, but instead she was forced to chase me down and ask if I was going to school. After that day I never cut class again.

I made a huge transformation that year and it showed in everything that I did. When I first got to my grandmother's I was broken, but now the pieces were coming back together. I remember when I first moved in with her and she had asked me what color I wanted to paint my room. I said black. Of course, she said no. At the time I thought, "Why would you ask me what I want if you're just going to say no?" It wasn't until she asked me again, almost a year later that I understood. This time I picked the color peach.

With my help, too, the girls' basketball program was rejuvenated that year. My teammates would joke about me being the star and them being my sidekicks. That season I would have several fifty-point games and would start to make a name for myself. Basketball gave me confidence and brought me out of my shell. I also started to cultivate some good friendships outside of the projects' playgrounds. Queens Lutheran gave me a glimpse outside of where I lived. My mind was now opened to a life away from the graffitied walls, the urine-filled elevators, and the roach infested apartments.

Out of the two hundred students that attended the school, about thirty or so were black and very few lived in the projects. Whenever I would visit the homes of my friends their pools and other luxuries amazed me. My grandmother would always remind me that if I ever wanted any of that, I would have to work hard and stay in school so that one day I could afford it. Her words had a way of sticking with me.

For the first time I understood what it felt like to be a part of a community. My classmates and I would attend church on Sundays and feed the homeless one-day a week. My grandmother would rotate the days she would cook throughout the month with the other church members. The people we fed loved my grandmother, especially her cooking. They would always ask for her famous chili and whenever they did, she would blush every single time. It felt good to uplift other people and to give what we could. These experiences showed me that I didn't have to have the perfect family as long as I had someone who cared and someone who wanted to see me grow and succeed. I had a community who supported me and I would not let them down.

With the embarrassing moments and drunken tirades becoming distant memories, I no longer had to worry about being teased about the actions of my parents. No more coming home to find my mother drunk and asleep outside on the bench. No more curse words flying through the air as my parents argued. I no longer felt shame for the things that they did. I learned to walk with my head up and to avoid the temptation to hide. My time at Queens Lutheran was special, and it would shape my future.

During the summer before entering eighth grade, I had to take placement exams for high school. There was no way my grandmother was letting me go back into the public school system after seeing the progress I had made while attending private school. I had to pick three schools where I was interested in going. I chose St. Johns Prep, St. Agnes and Stella Maris. I figured I would end up at St. Johns because it was the closest, but little did I know that I would not end up going to any of these schools.

I started my summer just like I had the one before, on the basketball courts. I was looking forward to playing with the boys again. It was much different than playing with the girls from Queens Lutheran. One day, Reggie, the coach of the boy's team, called my house and told me he was getting some of the boys together. He wanted me to meet up with them the following day at the neighborhood elementary school park for a tournament he had entered us into. I was excited as always, and checked to see if my grandma would let me go. She said it would be fine.

I remember we played two games that day and it was very hot out, but our team was balling and we won both games. After winning the first game, Tyrone Green who was the head of our P.A.L. organization, called Reggie and me over and introduced us to an older Italian gentleman. After the introduction he said that I was an unbelievable talent and asked me where I had learned to shoot pull-up shots like that. I remember laughing, saying "Thank you!" and running off to continue playing with my friends. When we had finished our second game, I noticed that the man was gone.

Reggie then came up to me and said, "Chamique, that was Vincent Cannizzaro. He's the head coach from the women's powerhouse, Christ the King."

"Cool," I said, not thinking much of it.

That summer continued to blow by. My friends and I hit the hoop circuit and beat up on teams, especially when they'd play like girls. By contrast, I would give them straight buckets. Our biggest rivals were from the Queensbridge Housing Projects, which is the largest public housing development in North America. They were known for having produced some of the greatest players and M.C.s. They had this young kid, Michael Chatfield. Man! No one could guard him. His game was so smooth and deadly. Then they had Ron Artest, aka Ron Ron. We could not beat them, but there was always a crowd at those games.

Those were the days when we just all got out there and competed in whatever shoes we had. We were just having fun. I laugh now because I can recall spending countless hours trying my hardest to beat Michael Chatfield in one-on-one games, but I never could. That same summer Ron Ron and I played together at the Boys and Girls Club. Even though he was younger, when the boys would try to get rough with me, Ron would always have my back. That year he was my back up on our team. I can't remember for sure, but I'm pretty certain that we won the championship at the club.

The school year was due to start, and everyone was talking about what schools they had applied to and what they did all summer. I remember my coach, Mr. Maldonado, asking what high school I was going to. I said that I didn't know, but was probably headed to St. Johns Prep. We went on to discuss summer ball and I told him how I had played P.A.L. and met this coach from Christ the King. He got excited and said, "CTK is the best high school team in NYC. They send a lot of players to college, especially Division 1." This was all over my head at the time, but I could sense the man was ecstatic.

It must have been just about a few months later when I received a call from Tyrone Green from P.A.L saying that Mr. Cannizzaro would love for me to attend Christ the King. It sent a ripple down my body! The best high school for women's basketball wanted me to play there? I was doing my happy dance; that was, until I told my grandmother the news. She was not even a bit excited. I showed her some of their previous news articles and she wasn't impressed. Tyrone had told me that the school was more expensive than St. Johns, but that a wealthy family would sponsor my scholarship. That meant that my grandmother wouldn't have to pay anything for me to attend private school. I couldn't understand her hesitation.

One night at the dinner table we talked about it in depth. She said she didn't feel comfortable with someone paying for my school because when people do things like that, they think they own you. She also wasn't too excited that the school would require me to travel an hour each way on public transportation. Since I wasn't really a morning person, she wasn't so sure that I would even be on time. More importantly, she believed nothing was for free. We went back and forth for weeks. Even Tyrone and Reggie put their bid in and tried to talk with her, but still no "yes." I was frustrated and upset. I wondered if any part had to do with her son, my Uncle Thurman Holdsclaw, who was a high school standout and was offered several Division 1 scholarships. He'd attended Power Memorial and had a great career. Maybe he had a bad experience?

Finally, I begged. I made a promise that I would make good grades and be on time for school. And one day, she said the magic word. I immediately called Tyrone Green to say that I could go. I filled out all the paperwork and testing information shortly after. A few months later I was officially accepted into the high school and I was more than thrilled. I finished out the school year solid academically, and won the Division in basketball at Queens Lutheran.

During the summer before starting high school nothing really changed, and this was a good thing. My brother and I continued to enjoy the stability our grandmother had brought into our lives. My dad still made his visits and supported us as best as he could, while my mom was still going through her addiction issues. I was playing softball that summer, but Mr. Cannizzaro wanted me to come out for the Amateur Athletic Union (A.A.U) practice for the NY Liberty Belles. My Aunt Anita and Uncle George had agreed to pick me up from CTK if I took the bus over. I had just finished my softball game and was wearing some tan khaki shorts and a lavender P.A.L shirt. From there, I went straight to basketball practice.

Right away I noticed that the way these girls played the game was more organized and structured. I also met someone who would remain my good friend, Malikah Willis, who is currently the assistant coach at West Virginia University. We became close since we were the only two African American girls on the team. We spoke the same language. She loved basketball just as much as I did, and we were both able to score in a hurry.

After practice, Mr. Cannizzaro came over and spoke to my aunt and uncle about me playing summer ball, but all my aunt and uncle were concerned about was my attire: those khaki shorts and that lavender shirt! I did not look the part, but it didn't matter to me. I was out there doing what I loved. After practice they took me to Modell's to buy me some basketball shorts, a few tops and socks. My aunt and uncle didn't have any kids of their own; they had found a brain tumor in my aunt during her last year of high school and because of this she had to endure many surgeries. She didn't want to have any children of her own because she was afraid that they would have disabilities due to her condition and all the medications required to keep her immune system strong. Despite her struggles, she has been a lifelong blessing to me. She and George were a huge part of the village that wound up raising us.

Meanwhile, my grandmother wasn't very happy about the money the family would have to pay for AAU, but she agreed. My dad was excited about the opportunity and wanted to help. He paid the fees and I was able to participate in my first tournament with girls outside of school. Some of us would be together for four years watching each other grow through high school. I bonded easily with my teammate Danielle Burch, with whom I had much in common.

We girls nicknamed Mr. Cannizzaro "U-turn Vinnie," because he was always getting us lost on the way to games. We traveled in a big van to different states to compete and also attended summer camp at Eastern Invitational in New Jersey. This camp was a really big deal and something that everyone had looked forward to. It was the chance to compete against the best players within the Tri-State area. It not only allowed us to show off our skills, but helped prepare us for future games. Never mind the fun adventures we would have so far away from home. All we could talk about was basketball, music, and boys—typical teenage girls.

It was just a few weeks until I would officially be a high school freshman. I recall sitting down with my grandmother and ordering my uniforms. She went over my options, which included a blue, maroon, and gray skirt and various sweaters and shirts with the CTK emblem on them. The great thing about CTK was that you were able to wear any button-down collared shirt that you wanted. So we could express our-selves individually without breaking the school's dress code. We decided to order one of each colored skirt and to head to Macy's for the button-down shirts and shoes.

Shoes were always the hardest things for me to find. I wore a size 13.5 women's at the time and back in the 90s, shoes in that size were nearly impossible to find. Luckily, the style back then was Timberland and Bass boat shoes so I was able to find those in men's sizes. Boy, did I luck out! If I had to wear those clown-like saddle shoes in my size, I would have probably gotten teased much more. I've always had big feet and it's often the first thing people comment on when meeting me. So there I was, a freshman in high school, wearing the same size shoes as my father. But as school was fast approaching, my feet were the least of my worries. I was consumed with how I would fit in socially and how I would fulfill all the promises I had made to my grandmother.

SECOND
QUARTER

CHAPTER 3

Growing Pains

I remember my first day of high school like it was yesterday, and this is because my good friend, Rashad Meade, won't ever let me forget it. My grandmother had decided that she wanted to ride the bus with me the first day. I agreed, but only until we transferred buses. It was bad enough that she was trying to make friends for me at most of the functions we went to; I didn't want her riding with me all the way to school, too.

Standing in front of Blimpie's at Queens Plaza, waiting on the Q67 that would take us to Christ the King were a bunch of kids, including my friend Rashad. Of course, I was the only one with their grandmother. Rashad lived in the Queensbridge Housing Projects; he had played against me that summer in a basketball league at D.S Park. As I glanced to the back of the bus, I noticed Rashad waving at me, thinking I was going to go to the back and sit with him. Instead, however, I sat with my grandmother and ducked my head. As the bus was in transit, making its stops and pick-ups of other students, I was still the only one with a parent or guardian. I lost all my "cool points" that day.

As I got off the bus and crossed the street, finally alone, I remember staring down the hill at the school. I remember walking into homeroom 1F and I noticed Morley, who my grandmother had introduced me to while completely embarrassing me at a recent orientation. We sat next to each other and became fast friends. As the year went on, Morley nicknamed me "The Candy Girl" because I would always have sweets in my locker. As a way to make extra money I would sell candy to students outside of my locker. I would buy a pack of gum for 50 cents and sell each piece for a quarter, making a profit. I really thought I was doing big business at the time.

My transition to CTK went better than I expected. I made friends at school and on the buses I rode. My bus crew and I would meet everyday at Queens Plaza. We used to decide while heading home if we would take the 7:20 or 7:40 bus the next day. We didn't use cell phones at the time so we would talk about our plans for the next day the night before.

Basketball was great too. It helped that I knew the upperclassmen from the basketball team. We were all looking forward to the upcoming season and carrying on the winning tradition. At our first basketball meeting with all the players, the coaches from both teams talked about the program and the history. They also talked about how we were expected to conduct ourselves. They wanted the best for us on and off of the court. I had already played with Danielle Burch for AAU over the summer, so we were ecstatic about being on junior varsity together. We were going to continue to be the one-two combo we'd been all summer. I couldn't wait for the season to start. But my plans weren't exactly the coaches' plans.

Once the meeting was over Mr. Cannizzaro had pulled me to the side and told me that they were going to put me on varsity instead of junior varsity. I must have looked at him like he was speaking in a foreign language. I said, "Mr. C, are you sure? I really want to play with my age!" He said, "Chamique, you are good enough and this is going to make you a better player." I went home and told my grandmother who was of course, very proud. My Aunt Anita and Uncle George were also happy. I, on the other hand, was trying to figure out if I would ever play. It was an honor I should have been happy about, but in the back of my head I wasn't sure if it was what I wanted. My grandmother knew that this was upsetting to me and kept reminding me that God has a plan. As usual she would be right. The following day, we had another meeting to pick our basketball numbers. I was a big Magic Johnson fan, so I picked No.32. I held my breath as everyone went around the room picking their desired number, hoping that no one would pick the number I wanted. Magic had always amazed me as a kid. Watching the way he handled the ball and how tall he was, I couldn't take my eyes of the television when he played. I loved how he could get rebounds and go coast to coast to score, or pass off for an amazing assist. He was a player that created action, and I wanted to play just like him. He didn't have to wait for anyone else; he could do it all.

I went home that night, and as always my grandmother, brother and I had dinner together. I remember telling my grandmother about the number that I had picked. She told me, "Chamique, you should have chosen No.23 for the 23rd Psalm, not Michael Jordan." I listened to her and laughed. "Come on, grandma! I'm getting number 32."

Once the uniforms had arrived for our fitting, we were all excited. It meant that games were right around the corner. I couldn't wait to get out there with the No.32 on my back. Coach Bob Mackey handed them out to all the girls. But when it came my turn to receive my jersey, it had No.23 on it. I looked up at him with a confused expression and told him that I wrote down and had chosen No.32. Knowing I was disappointed, he went on to explain how No.32 was too large. Nakia Hill was going to have to wear that jersey instead. I was crushed but had to accept it. Nakia was our star and I was just a freshman. She was a 6'3 pro-type power forward who had led our team the past few years. She was a phenomenal athlete. I remember watching her leg press the whole rack in our weight room during a workout. Every major college was recruiting Nakia. Schools loved that she was really tough but with a nice touch around the basket.

So, it turned out that I didn't get the number that I wanted and that was that. I remember saying to myself that if I couldn't be like Magic; I was going to be like Mike. When I told my grandmother about the number incident she said, "See! You were supposed to have that number for the 23rd Psalm."

And in truth, that number turned out to be perfect for me. I would go on to repeat the 23 Psalm to myself before every game throughout my career. It was even the subject for my first Nike commercial:

The Lord is my shepherd, I shall not want; He makes me lie down in green pastures. He leads me beside still waters; He restores my soul. He leads me in paths of righteousness for His name's sake. Even though I walk through the valley of the shadow of death, I fear no evil; for You are with me; Your rod and Your staff, they comfort me. Surely goodness and mercy shall follow me all the days of my life; and I shall dwell in the house of the Lord forever.

For me, it was my Protection Prayer and reminded me that no matter what I went through, God would be there for me.

My personality was really starting to develop as I got to meet and know the new people in my life. The unforgettable morning rides to school with Rashad on the Q67 got my heart rate up and ready to tackle the day. We would talk about music and crack jokes. My favorite class during that time was History. This was mainly because it was something factual. I was interested in knowing how things came to be. I also loved it because I had a photographic memory and always did well on exams. My teacher, Mr. Brown, was always very helpful and when he taught he had a way of pulling us in. He made learning new information fun instead of a chore.

With the season about to start, there were several articles being written about us, the Defending State Champs. We were ranked No.2 in the country and there was a huge buzz about our team. We had five players on our team that were going to go on to play high level division one basketball. We were lead by Nakia Hill (University of Georgia), Christine Fryer (Fairfield University), and Keisha McFadgion (Arizona State University). We were an exceptionally talented team and couldn't wait to show it. Practice was of course intense. Physically I was able to keep up, but it was my first time really being *taught* the game of basketball. It was obvious that I was a step behind. I felt like I was running top speed, but never got anywhere. Still, I kept my head up and just worked harder. I wanted to learn all I could from my teammates and coaches.

I remember times when the upperclassmen would try to intimidate me because I was the youngest. One specific time Malikah Willis had fouled Nakia Hill and she got really upset and swore. Coach Mackey had told us to double down on Hill in preparation for our next opponent. As we proceeded to trap her, she elbowed me in my mouth out of frustration. I tumbled to the ground, my mouth full of blood. The coaches checked on me, but what could they do? She was our star player. I sucked it up and saw it as a learning experience. I got the brunt of most frustrations that year; I guess it was my rite of passage on varsity.

Meanwhile, there was another part of me that was getting prepared for the future. During my freshmen year I didn't play much. After some games I'd be irate that I could have been on junior varsity, working on my game instead of riding the bench. Although at the time I didn't see it, I now know that Mr. C. was preparing me mentally. I learned unforgettable lessons from this.

Our team practiced either from 3:45 p.m. to 5:45 p.m. or 5:45 p.m. to 7:45 p.m. On those days when it was a late practice I would shower then wait for the bus hoping they would run on time. I would remind myself that this was the sacrifice I had to make to be a part of such a great team. Sometimes I wouldn't get home until 9:45 p.m. My grandmother would wait up for me and would come sit with me if I was still hungry.

Cold months were the worst. It would be freezing cold and there I would be, waiting for the bus while everyone else's parents picked them up. Waiting in that cold when I didn't even get to play made my frustrations kick in. To this day this is exactly why I respect everyone on any team: all the players put the same work in during practice, yet not everyone will get the glory.

One time, my grandmother, Anita and Uncle George all came to a big game of ours at CTK during a Christmas tournament. I remember my family talking about how well we played and how one of the girls on my team played especially well. As usual, I had simply sat on the bench and my blood boiled as they talked. I said to them, "Who cares, because I don't! Now can we stop talking about basketball." I remember everyone in the car sitting in silence as we headed back home to Astoria. I sat in the back seat and cried. My grandmother would always say, "Chamique, don't worry. You're only a freshman. Your time will come, just be patient and pray." Although there were times when I acted like I wasn't listening, I always hung onto her words. After letting go of the built up frustrations, I took my grandma's advice and tried to make the best of the situation. I worked really hard in school, so she was proud of that. I started to appreciate the experience.

My team played away games in some hostile environments, such as Cardinal O'Hare, Downingtown in Pennsylvania, as well as St. John's Vianney in New Jersey. I took my first plane trip that year to Lake Charles, Louisiana. I somehow managed to break my team bag, so my grandmother and I searched up and down for an affordable piece of luggage for that trip. After looking and looking, finally she found me a purple and blue Sierra bag from Macy's. At LaGuardia, I didn't know if I should check my bag or carry it on. I had arrived late, so in order to not miss my flight I decided to take the duffle bag with me on the plane. Once I had finally made it to the plane a few of the seniors asked me why I had such a big bag with me. They told me that I should have checked it. They laughed at me and at the fact it was my first time flying.

Mr. Mackey assisted me with my bag. He told me everything would be alright and shoved my bag into the overhead bin. Halfway through the flight I fell asleep, and when I woke up we were on the ground. When we arrived at the hotel I called my grandma and told her how I wasn't scared and how it was no big deal and cautiously skipped the part about the bag. As always, she told me to be thankful that I was safe and to appreciate the opportunity to have these types of experiences. I listened on the other end of the phone as her words comforted me. She believed in me and my talent. She knew that I would one day have my opportunity to showcase my skills.

My day finally came when our star, Nakia Hill, was suspended for a game. Finally, my number was called. Yes! I was going to get to start in the CHSAA semifinal game against St. Francis Prep, our rival. I was so nervous I was shaking. Coach Cannizzaro came over and talked to me, trying to give me some sort of confidence. I listened to his words, but the stare he got was a blank one as I tried in vain to focus. The game that night was poetry in motion. I even got my picture in the local paper and I must have thanked God a hundred times. As the season came to an end, we capped it off by winning the state championship.

Back on the home front, I had come to grips with the fact that my parents would never get us back. My mom couldn't kick her bad habit. My grandmother could sense my anger when I had to ask her to sign a permission slip for a trip. She said I would have to get in touch with my mother. I couldn't understand the whole thing because my grandmother was my guardian, just not on paper. That was what prompted my grandmother to ask my mom if she could adopt me. My mom didn't like this idea at all. She went into a rage saying that I was her child and that she wasn't going to let my grandmother take me. She even made it a point to come over to my grandmother's house to further express her discontent. After seeing her disrespect my grandmother, I was done. I no longer wanted any kind of relationship with her. I remember asking her why she even cared, considering she wasn't there for me anyway. I tried to explain that she might as well just sign the paper because it would be easier for everyone.

At this point my mom was still a functional alcoholic. She would go to work every day for the city. She was actually always employed with a good city job, but it was what she did during non-work hours that caused the demise of our family. At that time I couldn't remember a weekend when she didn't drink. I'm not sure what changed her mind or how it happened, but she and my grandmother, along with the help of our social worker, resolved the situation. There was a clear record by the state that I was being raised by my grandmother and because I did not carry my father, William C. Johnson's, last name, guardianship was granted. I felt at peace. I no longer needed to ask her for anything. My grandmother was officially all the parent I needed.

That summer after my freshman year was all about basketball. Between AAU and playing with the guys in my neighborhood, I was always busy and with a basketball in my hand. I really wanted to play on the P.A.L with a particular group of guys from my neighborhood. I would watch them out of my grandmother's apartment window, which directly looked into the court. One day my grandmother said to me, "Chamique, I'm going to ask them boys can you play with them." I panicked and told her no, but she did anyway. When she returned after talking to them, she informed me that they said I could go and try out. I put my sneakers as quick as I could and headed downstairs with the speed of the wind. As I approached the court, they all stared at me. I nervously went and talked with the coach, who told me to do drills with the other boys. I did well and was better than half of the guys out there. It felt great to be back on the court with the guys. I loved playing with the girls at my school, but there was nothing like playing on the courts in my neighborhood. This was home.

At the end of practice he told everyone to get into a circle. He went on to say how he has never had a girl on his team and wasn't sure what to do. So he decided that he would have everyone vote to see if I could be on the team. The guys all moved together within their own circle and shortly thereafter, the coach emerged with the verdict: No.

Back at my apartment, I opened the door with anger and instantly my grandmother asked me what happened. I yelled and told her that it was a dumb idea to ask them if I could play. I asked her with rage why she would do that. I went into my room and cried and cried. I was so disappointed. Even though I was good, it was the fact that I was a girl that kept me off of the team. I remember thinking to myself that at least he should have made the decision himself. In my eyes that coach was a coward. It wasn't my fault that I was better than half the boys on his team. I ended up linking up with another P.A.L. team, but we weren't very good.

Luckily, I had the AAU circuit ahead of me to look forward to. My AAU team's first stop was to Amarillo, Texas for Nationals. Wow! It was my first time in Texas and I had no idea what to expect. The heat and the cowboys were like nothing I had ever experienced. To me, Texas was like one of the old western movies that I had enjoyed as a kid. It reminded me of the character Calamity Jane, but in living color instead of on television.

I was really growing up and on this trip I took a new step into womanhood for me: I started my period. I remember waking up in pain and confiding in my roommate Danielle. Danielle got up out of bed and took me to her mother's room. Luckily for me, Mrs. Burch happened to be one of our chaperones for the trip. She called my grandmother to tell her and then gave me some pads. Being a good friend, Danielle instructed me about what to do. Later that day, Ms. Burch took me to the store and went over all of the various products with me. She told me that I would experience pain from time to time and to take some Advil when that occurred. She was so kind to me, hugging me and telling me that it would all be alright. While she was nice enough to explain that whole process to me, I never really got that traditional "birds and bees" talk from my grandmother. Instead, my grandmother simply just told me that since I had gone through those changes, I could get pregnant. Her famous line was, "Chamique, don't let the thing between your legs control your head."

She didn't have much to worry about because I wasn't thinking about boys like that yet. To me, they were just my friends, but I did notice that they were starting to like me. But what I saw growing up in the projects made me not want to be liked by them. I had some friends who had gotten pregnant at just 14 or 15 years old. I could not imagine something like that in my life: all I wanted to do was run around the streets and be active. I didn't want anything to come in between me and my first love, basketball. Another thing that hit home and impacted me was the fact that my mother had me at 19. I saw what being a young mother did to her and didn't want to end up like that.

After dealing with my girly changes in Amarillo, we played great and finished in the top ten at AAU nationals. I was on fire and proud to be rocking my grey and black Jordan 7s. When you are that young, you really believe that the shoes make you play better. On top of that, I was No.23. I felt as if I truly channeled the spirit of MJ when I played.

Once we got home from that trip, school was right around the corner. My family had a barbecue at my Aunt Maggie's house in Roslyn for Labor Day. It was such a peaceful place where she lived on Long Island. I remember visiting the beautiful park that was right across the street from her home. It was a far cry from the beat up elevators and graffiti-marked walls where I lived. Whenever we went to her house it was like a vacation. We would go to the park and throw the Frisbee around and play touch football. I was really looking forward to the school year so I could share my summer travel stories and all that I'd experienced.

CHAPTER 4

Making Strides

Sophomore year had finally begun and we were ranked No.3 in the nation by every publication that covered girl's basketball. This was the year that I knew I would be a starter. Well, let me rephrase that: this was the year that I *wanted* to be a starter. None of the coaches had actually told me, but every publication was saying we would surprise a lot of people if I could produce at the varsity level. I was confident that I could. At the same time, I didn't know how I would gel with the girls on varsity because they spent the summer player together while I'd been with my own age group.

I knew from the very beginning that I was going to have to go hard. The comforting thing was that I knew all of the girls on the team because I had carried their bags last year. I was also, of course, their No.1 cheerleader last season while I sat there forlorn on the bench.

From the start I was focused. I gained the coaches trust, as well as that of my teammates. I guess they realized that I could actually help them win. They played me at power forward, but I would get the rebound, dribble up the court on the break and go coast to coast. In my head I didn't want to play inside, but this is where the coach had me. I didn't care how I got on the floor; just that I was there.

I was not your pro-type power forward. My game was different. I could dribble like a guy; inside out moves, behind the back, between the legs and probably with better handles than most point guards. My rebounding ability was uncanny. I could leap and grab the ball out of the air right off of the rim. I guess it came from playing with the boys: if I didn't get rebounds playing with them I might not get the ball at all. My instincts were great, and I stood at 6'1 after a slight growth spurt I'd hit after freshman year.

Our team beat everyone that stood in front of us. I thought we had a large crowd at games the year before, but this year there were even more people in the stands. It was overwhelming to run out to a crowd of screaming fans. All the hype began to be a distraction for me. My assistant coach, Bob Mackey, had to pull me aside to talk to me about the importance of taking care of the books, too. I was slacking a bit and letting basketball consume all of my time. My grandmother sat me down and told me that if I wanted to change my life, I would have to do it through academics. She said that no college would ever take me if my grades weren't good. She told me that if I continued to apply myself I could write my own ticket. Those few words from both of them would be the last time either of them had to talk with me about my schoolwork. I didn't want anything to stand between me and the court.

During my time playing at CTK the coaches didn't allow players to get letters from colleges until after freshman year. Now a sophomore, I started getting lots of interest letters from various colleges. My first letters came from Auburn and Colorado, and I started wearing their school colors. I also read their media guides over and over until I knew all the players on each team. I was so excited at the thought of getting the opportunity to play past high school. Out of my immediate family, I would be the first to go to college.

Due to my individual success, more was expected from me. Practices had become more grueling. I would finish up, head to the showers and then catch the bus headed back to Astoria just like the previous year. I was thankful that my stop was the last one on both lines, because there were several times when I dozed off. Who knows what city I would have ended up in if the driver had not woken me up. But this was what I wanted. This was what I agreed to do.

In the days leading up to a big game at CTK versus St. Francis Prep, my grandmother came into my room to discuss something with me. She told me that my mother wanted to come and watch one of my games. I was totally against it and broke out in a rage. I told my grandmother that if my mother came to my game and was under the influence of alcohol, I would walk off the court. My grandmother assured me that she would have things under control. I could only imagine my mother yelling, "*I'm the one that taught Chamique how to play ball*"—that was her favorite line, but it wasn't true.

When we were growing up in Jamaica, Queens my parents loved to take us to a park that was near Goose Pond. They especially loved to play street handball, so while they would play, we kids would play around on the swings or on the softball field. One day at the park this kid who happened to be my mother's friend Linda's son asked me if I wanted to play basketball. I agreed. I couldn't reach the basket yet, so I would shoot using the typical two-hand underhand method. Many young kids try to make a basket this way. It was bad, but I would try and try until I touched the goal. That being said, my mom loves to tell people that *she* put the basketball in my hand. I never argue with her about it anymore. Instead, I just laugh it off. But I trusted my grandmother, so I said fine in regards to my mother attending the game, and asked ever so nicely not to let her embarrass me.

It was soon game day and I ran out to a packed gymnasium and a roaring crowd. St. Francis Prep was our biggest rival in our CHSAA league. Our games were typically close until the fourth quarter, when our conditioning would wear them out. Coach Cannizzaro had just called a timeout and all I could focus on was my mother, grandmother, and my little brother all sitting next to each other. My mom looked calm, but I was skeptical. I glanced over to my grandmother who gave me a wink, letting me know everything was under control. During that game's halftime break I was just off somewhere else mentally because I couldn't believe my mother had showed up to one of my games, never mind that she was also sober. To make the night even more amazing, after the break, I started to warm up and there was my dad sitting with them. We went on to win the game that night, but for me it felt more like winning a championship. I was so happy to have my family there supporting me. For once, it wasn't about their issues. It was about me. Sadly, there would not be many times like this, but the moments that we did have I cherished. I learned a long time ago in Alateen meetings that there is no such thing as a perfect family dynamic. There's no *Cosby Show* in real life.

As sophomore year moved along I buried myself in school and basketball. People started to refer to me as "The Super Sophomore." My teammates loved me and their parents cheered and supported me as if I was their own. My grandmother had seen my growth, but she also knew that I had still had more work to do. She had to deal with my stereotypical teenager tantrums. And beyond that, my more severe anger issues.

I was once promised something that didn't happen. I got really upset and tore my room upside down as I cried and cried. This was not the first time I had lost it, but I remember this time because of my grandmother's words. After my episode she sat me down and said, "Chamique, if you have this anger and stuff built up inside I'd rather you take it out inside of this house or on the basketball court. Don't be in the street doing this stuff and acting up." She then went on, "Secondly, you have to learn to pray and allow God to help you let go of that anger." She hugged me and told me that she loved me.

I went back to my room, got on my knees and thanked God for having her in my life. I prayed for my family and asked him to ease the pain in my heart. I knew I had developed an issue with people promising me something and then not following through. My parents' lies drove me to want to do more for myself because I never wanted to have to rely on anyone else to fulfill my happiness. I couldn't bear to be disappointed. I didn't want a promise to be made that could not be kept. Their lies became a gift and a curse.

We finished the basketball season ranked No.1 by the *U.S.A Today* High School Basketball poll. I was named a *Parade* All-American and won my second state championship. I averaged 19.9 points and 12 boards per game. I also ended the school year academically with a B average. We had an awesome team that year. It wasn't just a single person effort. We had Malikah Willis (University of Iowa), Kristen Fraser (Loyola), and Tammi McGlynn (George Washington University), among others.

To celebrate our all out success, the team wanted to head over to The Bridge. I had heard stories about this place but had never been there. It was located in the Howard Beach/Rockaway area. This was where a lot of my teammates were from. I knew that if I asked my grandmother to go, she would have said no, especially because of the race issues that had been all over the news.

At CTK it wasn't about race; we were a family. I remember one of my teammates saying there are crazy people everywhere, but that she and her family did not think like that. I knew and understood that, but my grandma would never want to hear it. I was her baby. Even in our own neighborhood I was never allowed to stay at a friend's house. She would say, "Your friends are more than welcome to come over and spend the night here." As I got older I better understood why she did this. There is too much that goes on in the news, and you never know what happens in other people's houses.

I knew my grandmother would not let me go to The Bridge and told the team. They suggested I ask if I could stay at Danielle's house. The Burch family lived about 15 minutes from us in Sunnyside, and they would often sit with my grandmother at our games. So if there was any chance of me getting to go, this was my best shot. When I called and begged her to stay with Danielle and her family, she finally gave in and said yes. She had no idea that I would actually be at The Bridge with the rest of my teammates.

It was my first high school party. When we arrived, a friend of my teammates let us into the club. We danced through the night and I drank alcohol for the first time. It was a Long Island Iced Tea. Though all I had was one drink, we had so much fun. Malikah and I were the only black girls in the whole entire club, but we didn't care. Everyone kept congratulating us on our success. Amidst all of the fun, I kept thinking about how I always got caught when I lied to my grandmother. But this would be the only time my grandmother didn't find out what I'd done.

With the season coming to an end I decided to try out for the school's track team and made it. I was always active and wanted something to keep me busy until AAU started in the summer. I went home to tell my grandmother, and as always she was supportive. I had told her that I needed to get some running shoes and she said she wasn't going to be spending $100; she already had to pay the related expenses for AAU and other summer activities. Finally, she gave in, but gave me a $50 limit. We went to Modell's to go shopping as we did for all my sporting equipment needs. I ended up picking out a pair of black Turntec running shoes.

When I returned to school the next day, the track coach looked at my sneakers like they were diseased. They weren't the Nikes she was use to seeing. For practice we had to run around our school eight times. Christ the King is a big school, with killer hills. As we ran around that day I couldn't figure out why I had decided to do this. I was miserable. I only lasted one day and decided it wasn't for me.

Besides, summer and AAU basketball practice was just around the corner. I was looking forward to going back to camp at The Eastern Invitational and playing games with my neighborhood crew. I was also ecstatic that my Uncle Thurman was coming to New York for the summer. He would always call me from Montana where he lived to give me basketball tips. He was my grandmother's only son and she loved him dearly.

I used to go into his room where my brother stayed and open up the boxes of his old college letters. I would compare them against mine to see if the same schools wanted both of us. He was actually a legend in Astoria. He played at the legendary Power Memorial High School in NYC. It was the same school where Kareem Abdul-Jabbar had gone. I used to marvel at the pictures of him playing on the same courts as some of New York City's greatest. I know he went to two Division 1 schools before ending up in Montana and playing for the Northern Montana Lights.

When he arrived, I will never forget how happy my grandmother was. Her baby boy was home. Thurman, who we all called TJ, didn't get home to New York as much as we all would have liked, so him being home that whole entire summer was a really big deal. I was excited because he was going to help me with my basketball skills. He had decided that he was going to help out and coach for one of the teams in the neighborhood while he was home. I was mad about this because it wasn't a team that I could play on. Instead, it was a team that all my guy friends were on. Even though he knew I was upset he did his best to help me and the other kids by putting us through workouts daily.

His individual goal for me that summer was for me to improve on my left hand and he rode me hard. He also taught me new moves: the inside-out crossover and inside out between the legs, which became two moves I perfected over the course of my career. He told me that New York ball players are known for their dribbling ability and being able to get to the basket effortlessly. He also insisted I work hard on trying to perfect my midrange game. He would have me dribble the ball full speed and pull up when he signaled. He would say, "Bam Bam, that pull up jumper has to be smooth like butter!" I had acquired the nickname "Bam Bam" from a very young age. Since I was active and aggressive, like the character on *The Flintstones*, TJ took it upon himself to give me that nickname.

I had started to get a lot of notice from college coaches, especially at camp. My teammates would constantly tease me. They would say things like, "I can't wait to play your team so the coaches might actually look at me since every time you step on the court, that's where their eyes go." I would just laugh it off. I knew I had a special gift, but I never wanted to be treated differently because of it. I always just wanted to be normal. So I kept joking around, keeping everyone loose and laughing.

Mr. C. told me early that summer that I wasn't going to be playing

AAU with my age group, but with the 16 and under instead. I was fine with that because I had played a year with the girls and I looked forward to the competition. But then a few weeks after school ended I was saddened by the news that our starting center, and my dear friend, Malikah Willis, would be moving to Ohio.

In an effort to get her to stay, a few of the parents told her mom that she could stay with them and finish out her last year at CTK. We had just finished the season ranking No. 1 and no one wanted her to leave. She told me that she thought it would be better for her if she went with her mother, and I had to accept that. As a friend, it hurt my heart to see her leave, but I wanted the best for her and her family. The worst part of it all was that she transferred to Trinity Garfield Heights, the basketball powerhouse in Ohio. I knew I would eventually end up playing against my good friend. Not having her on our team would be a huge loss, but I figured I'd worry about it when the time came. I decided it was best that I focus on playing well during the summer instead of things I could not control.

I really wanted to move to the small forward position and play on the wing, but my coaches felt I was better at the 4, especially since I was a great rebounder. I remember annoying my AAU coach, Jill Cook, so much that finally she played me on the perimeter. That was when I understood why she'd kept me at the 4. While I was on the perimeter, teams would double-team me and I was too far away from the basket to rebound so it would take away from my game. I still remember the look she gave me when she subbed me out. It was that facial expression that said, "See, I know what I'm talking about."

When AAU Nationals were over I headed back home and played with my friends, the boys from the neighborhood. This time however, it was with the team that had voted me out before. I was destined to prove that I belonged. I played like a madwoman that summer on the street courts of New York City and among all of those guys on my team there was me, the MVP. I was the best player that summer and to this very day, every time I see those guys that cut me I make sure to let them know what a mistake they made. They always laugh and say, "We were just getting you ready."

One of the biggest events of the summer within my neighborhood was Astoria Day. There would be a big cookout and the older guys would have a basketball tournament. It was a big deal to us kids. People would hang on the fences trying to get a look at who was on the courts. It was always about eight teams and the games would run all day long. This particular year I was really excited because my Uncle TJ would be playing. He really put on a show that summer. The best was when Astoria played Queensbridge in the final and my uncle put up 51 points. His 3-point shot was on fire and every time he drove, it seemed like it was a 3-point play. His performance was talked about for years, especially since it was against Queensbridge, who normally had our number in basketball. Afterwards, we all headed back to the apartment to celebrate.

Minutes after we got home there was a loud bang at the door and we peeked out to find my mother, drunk out of her mind. My grandmother didn't want to open the door and I hoped that she would just leave. Instead, my mom just kept yelling, "I want to see my baby brother." Finally, TJ hopped up and said, "Mom, I got this." He went and let my mom in. He told her to sit down and to stop all the yelling and cursing.

I remember sitting at the kitchen table looking at a woman I loved in my heart, but did not know. I remember Thurman asking her, "Why are you drinking so much, Bonnie?" She went off and started cussing and calling my grandmother all sorts of names. Thurman let her vent, but finally he told her she needed to get help. He told her like it was and said, "Look at you! Your kids and your own mother don't want to deal with you." While they were talking, my mother started to doze off, so my uncle said that he was going to take her somewhere. Of course my mom was rebellious, but couldn't resist my uncle because she was intoxicated and tired.

That day would change us forever. TJ took her to East Elmhurst Hospital, where my grandmother had been Chief of Medical Records for so many years. It was there that she went through the most difficult and painful detox experience of her life. I couldn't feel her pain, but what I could feel was relief in knowing that my mom was not out there on the streets. When she would get drunk she would become belligerent and violent. I always feared we would get a phone call saying that someone had hurt her or that she was dead. But as I felt this relief, my brother's heart was saddened. All he ever wanted was to be with my mother. No matter what she did or said he unconditionally loved her.

I'm proud and relieved to say that since that summer's night in 1993, my mom has not had one drink. Our relationship is now a great one and I'm amazed by her strength. I was the oldest. I lived through her struggles and had to grow up fast because of it. Some of the things that I saw, no child should ever see, but those things made me a stronger person and who I am today. I thank God everyday for giving her life back.

My grandmother couldn't thank TJ enough. He just said, "Mom, I didn't want to see my sister dead. Enough was enough." He went back to his life in Havre, Montana, but the impact he made on our family and in the community that summer was immeasurable. Uncle TJ truly became my hero that year.

CHAPTER 5

Getting Ready

With my junior year beginning, I had to start getting my academic affairs in order. Although I was doing well in school, I hadn't taken the SATs yet. I heard horror stories of great athletes who had the grades but lacked the required SAT score in order to be admitted into school. I had won outstanding player at Eastern Invitational Basketball Camp the previous summer and I was awarded a scholarship that paid for me to take the Princeton Review Course. This would help to prepare me for the SATs. I had to attend the course for 12 weeks every Saturday, at two different locations, for 3 hours per day. I also had to start thinking about colleges I might like to attend. The upcoming season was quickly approaching and before I knew it, I was consumed by practice and games.

The atmosphere was different without Malikah's silly humor and it was felt on the court. We also really missed her size and abilities. We had a tough schedule ahead of us, but before we played any games, we had to get on the same page as a team. My assistant coach, Mr. Mackey, was extra tough on me during practice. His excuse was that they weren't going to give me calls in the game. After days of this I became aggravated and the next thing I knew I had pitched the ball full court out of frustration. This was my first time ever doing something like that outside the walls of my home. I was tired of players fouling me and undercutting me without any calls being made. I was also worried that I would get hurt or injured during practice.

Mr. Mackey just looked at me and told me to leave if I wanted. I started to walk to the locker room and kicked the trashcan by the door. I went in, shed a few tears, and came back out. Coach Mackey asked if I was okay and I said yes. The practice continued. That day I realized that the people who care have to be tough on you at times in order to get you ready for what lies ahead. Coach Mackey was the type who didn't take any nonsense and I respected that. He would get in my face and yell, but that was his way of getting me fired up. Mr. Cannizzaro, on the other hand, was laid back and more like a father figure. He just wanted everyone to be happy. In the end I had two great coaches who really complemented one another well.

Just before the season started my Princeton Review class finished. This was convenient because I didn't have to worry about juggling both. I was scheduled to take the SAT in a few weeks so I was now able to focus my attention on ball. I started out just as I had left off the season before. I was playing well. In an effort to slow me down this season, players started double-teaming me during games. This meant that I had to work on passing out of traps. We had lost a few games at the start of the season. The opposing teams made it especially difficult for me by running gimmick defenses, such as a box and one. We worked hard to make the adjustments necessary because our team had changed greatly with the loss of Malikah.

Back on the home front, my mom was doing well in rehab and wanted me to come and see her. I told her that I needed some more time to work through some issues. It was hard for me because I had seen her leave rehab once before, only to turn around and have a drink less than a month later. I guess I just didn't want to get my hopes up too high. She would write and tell me how she loved reading the articles written about me in the paper.

My mom was also proud that I had been given an opportunity to write a monthly column for *USA Today* about my life as a highly recruited athlete. They had picked one boy and one girl who played for top high school programs. My friends thought I was so cool because of this. The boy that they had chosen was Trajan Langdon, who had committed to playing collegiate ball at Duke. Within each entry we would talk about our lives as high school athletes and the things we went through with our teams. This was a new and exciting experience for me.

That same year my team took a trip to Palos Verdes, California. They had a star player, Mimi McKinney, who was on everyone's All-American list, and I was really looking forward to the match up. I remember getting off the plane and being beyond excited. The scenery was breathtaking! The palm trees and the ocean were so serene. It was the complete opposite of the hustle and bustle in my New York City life. So I soaked it up and enjoyed every bit of it.

The day of the game I woke with butterflies in my stomach. I was about to go head to head with one of the best players in the country, someone I really looked up to. Mimi McKinney was an athletic 2/3 player and was highly recruited by all the major colleges. Even though I had those butterflies, once that jump ball occurred, I was ready to play. We played our hearts out and ended up winning the game. Afterwards, the other team invited my team to a party at one of their houses. We knew our coaches wouldn't let us go, so we took a vote and decided to sneak out.

The party was great. It was packed with other athletes from different schools who played various sports. We had a blast meeting new people. Like many parties in high school, alcohol was brought into the equation. I remember having a few drinks in order to fit in; I didn't want to be the odd man out. Drinking alcohol was never very appealing to me, given the situation with my parents. I guess growing up around alcoholics will make you that way. But I found myself caught up in trying to be cool and I didn't use my head. This was one situation where I was the follower versus the leader.

It turned out that someone had told our coaches where we were and they decided to pop in on us. We got into so much trouble that night.

Our coaches really ripped into the upperclassmen. They told us that they were very disappointed in us and if anything would have happened, they were the ones who would have been held responsible. I'm thankful nothing happened that night. It was exactly the learning experience I needed. I risked my future for a single selfish moment.

A few weeks after our unforgettable trip to California, Mr. Cannizzaro wanted to take me to a game at the University of Connecticut, who was recruiting me to play at their school. I asked my grandmother and she said it was fine. Along with a few of my teammates, I took the drive with Mr. C. to Storrs, Connecticut. Mr. C. took me for a tour around the campus and I had a chance to check out the facilities. The University of Connecticut was in the Big East Conference and I had the opportunity to watch them play. I met superstars Rebecca Lobo and Kara Wolters. I was so thrilled! The long drive up to see the game was well worth it. The atmosphere was exciting, plus I was happy to be inside that day. It was freezing cold out, with snow on the ground. As we toured around, teeth chattering, I collected a few schedules and a poster to bring back and show my friends. I knew that UConn was going to be an awesome team, plus they had a commitment already from my friend and stellar guard, Nykesha Sales.

Meanwhile, the letters continued to pour in from all sorts of colleges. I was getting so many letters that at times they couldn't all fit in our mailbox. The mailman would have to leave them with a neighbor, or I would have to pick them up from the post office. It truly was a great feeling, but I had become more concerned with my SAT score. After receiving the results in the mail, I realized that I hadn't done well at all, and would have to retake it. Mr. Cannizzaro told me not to get discouraged about it, and told me that I would do well the second time around. I was disappointed in myself, but luckily I had taken it early enough and so was able to retake the test. I did this as soon as I could. This time around I did great and I was very happy because now I had options. These options would afford me the ability to change my life.

That season we didn't rank No.1, but we did rank in the USA Top 25. Once again, we won the state championship and I was named an All-American and All "Everything" in New York City. Now with the high school season being over, I had to transition my thoughts and focus toward college. The stress of potentially having a test score come between me and my future was officially over. Recruiting had begun in full force, and coaches could now call my home and interact with me, and I will admit, it was a lot to handle. As always, my grandmother was extremely supportive. She just wanted me to take my time and make a good decision. She also didn't want me to think solely about basketball because she knew that would come easy. My grandmother suggested that I look at the overall picture: the number of undergrad students at the university, academic success, school support and active alumni. I had a lot to take into account for a 17-year-old. The decision would affect me for the rest of my life.

As the school year ended, my mom had completed her program at a rehabilitation facility in Staten Island. I was so proud of her and although I could see a change in her, I still didn't want to get ahead of myself. I could not afford any more disappointment. Since she was on the right path, my grandmother asked us once again if we wanted to go and live with her. I didn't want that and elected to stay with my grandmother. My brother had decided to leave however. I was sad because Davon and I were so close, but he was younger and still had that connection to her. I always knew that if she truly got better he would eventually leave. I remember going to visit my mom's new place. It was in St. George, which was not far from the Staten Island Ferry. It was a nice cozy three-bedroom townhouse. But I hated the fact that if you didn't drive, you had to take a forty minute ferry ride from Manhattan.

A few days later I received a phone call from Mr. C. asking if he could take my grandmother and me out for a bite to eat. After asking my grandmother, I told him yes. He wanted to meet regarding the recruiting process. At dinner he explained to my grandmother how the process could be grueling and how I could be spending hours talking on the phone. He proceeded to make a few suggestions on how we could handle this. He thought it was in my best interest to pick six schools that I was sincerely interested in. I would only take the phone calls from the schools that I had chosen and shut down communication with all of the others. It sounded like a great idea, so my grandmother and I agreed.

Next, it would just be a matter of gathering information and figuring out which schools I wanted to attend. My six choices were Penn State, Virginia, Tennessee, UConn, Purdue, and Ohio State. Even though I had put together this list, all sorts of schools would still call my house. We constantly had to tell coaches that I was not interested in their programs.

This had to be one of the craziest summers. I knew I had a big decision to make and I wanted to think carefully about it. I contemplated all of my options and what I thought to be important in a school. My friends and everyone else from the neighborhood would put their two cents in. It seemed like everywhere I went, someone wanted to talk about basketball and offer their opinions on where they thought I should go. I would politely listen. To get away from it all I would go and play pickup in my projects with the boys. We would play for hours on end and I would dominate, for the most part. I wasn't able to jump as high as some of them, but I still found a way to score. I remember one day when Keith Leslie, a childhood friend that I had grown up playing ball with and some of the guys were just dunking and trying new moves. So I joined in and tried to dunk too. After about seven tries, I recorded my first dunk. My boys went crazy! I remember during an AAU game that same summer at CTK I tried to go for a dunk on a fast break. I missed and the whole crowd went crazy. From that point on, whenever I got the ball on a break, the crowd would scream, "Dunk it!" My miss was an in and out. Had I made it, I would have really been the talk of the town. I was all about breaking records and doing things no one before me had done.

At summer camp I was constantly receiving messages from different schools. It seemed like I was always on the phone talking to a college coach. My games were packed with coaches, family, and camp-goers wanting to get a glimpse of me in action. I didn't let that overwhelm me too much. At that point, I had become used to the attention and I just made the best out of the situation. My friends were also getting recruited, so I would listen to their stories in order to take the attention off of me. I would of course also joke around and be silly because that was just me.

When I arrived back home from camp, TJ had called me and asked me about colleges. I proceeded to tell him my list. He went on to explain that Ohio State and Penn State should be taken off. He suggested this because he said that those schools were too big for me and that I would just get lost in the mix of thousands of other students. Although I didn't really understand, my grandmother told me that I should take that into account. I was a little annoyed because they were trying to tell me what to do and on top of that, I really liked Rene Portland and her staff who were with Penn State. Penn State was also in The Big 10, a competitive conference, and I was excited at the thought of playing at that level.

During the recruiting part of the process, my grandmother and I started to bump heads. She really understood that my choice would affect the rest of my life, but I just didn't understand that then. I remember telling her that I had to go and meet these people in order to see what it would be like. After going back and forth over control, one day I told my grandmother that I wanted to go live with my mother. God knows I loved my grandmother with all of my heart, but I think I got tired of how over protective she was of me. I was going into my senior year of high school and I still wasn't allowed to hang out late. If she did let me, it was only because I was out on the courts and she was able to see me from her window. She treated me like I was still a baby and I could not stand it. I called my mother and told her that I had packed up my stuff and was on my way to live with her in Staten Island. I knew it would be a longer commute to CTK during the next school year, but it didn't matter.

My grandmother told me that I would be back, but I didn't think so. I was okay with making this adjustment, so I selfishly disregarded my grandmother's feelings and headed to my mother's. My mom was doing great and our relationship was much better. I hadn't considered living with my father, but at the time he was still living in Queens and we saw him every chance we got. I knew I would miss my friends in Astoria, but I could easily make new ones. Basketball in NYC is like a universal language that everyone speaks. I could always find a game going on in the parks.

But what's that old saying? "Be careful what you wish for"? I moved in with my mom and brother and everything was going great in Staten Island. I had made some new friends. I also loved the extra time I got to spend with my brother. However, I hated my mom's rules, or should I say one of her rules. She believed that once you wake up in the morning, the very first thing you should do is get up, shower, brush your teeth, and get on with your day. In short, that meant no lying around. I thought she was crazy! What teenager wants to wake up early during their summer?

I was a growing young woman. It was summertime and I needed my rest. After listening to my mother complaining for about a week, I called my grandmother and apologized. I told her I was coming back home and when I walked through the doors on that hot summer's day she didn't hesitate to say, "I told you so." All I could do was hug her as we both laughed. After that she then sat me to say no matter which school I chose, she expected me to graduate in four years. My grandmother also made it very clear that I would not be transferring, so I had better get it right the first time. She knew that my whole future hinged on this decision. She saw beyond the future practices and games I would play. Her only concern was me graduating from college. She wanted to ensure that I would have a promising future outside of the sport I loved. My grandmother wanted more for me than I could have ever wanted for myself. She loved all of her grandchildren the same, but I was the first and because of that, we shared a special bond.

My grandmother always made it a point to tell me how proud she was of me. She used to say, "Chamique, sometimes I have to remember that you are not my child." In my heart and hers she was just as much my mother as I was her daughter and our bond reflected just that. I remember she would have me set the table for our big holiday dinners. She taught me where every utensil went and its use. She wanted to make sure I knew the proper etiquette so that I would be comfortable no matter where I went or what the situation. My grandmother would say, "Chamique, it's not where you are from, it's where you are going." I know the value of having structure, discipline, humility and self-worth because of her. She instilled all of the most important traits that make me, me.

I remember how excited she was the day that Davon and I were baptized. I was 12 and had a renewed joy in my heart for the Lord. I had been witness to how faith in Him could change one's life and for me there was no one more faithful than my grandmother. During the most difficult times, she encouraged me get on my knees and ask for the strength to endure. I knew God would never fail me and I was excited to commit my life to Him. But during the ceremony the candle fell on my hand and burned me. It hit my hand and fell to the floor and I apologized for my clumsiness. Pastor Myers then looked me in my eyes and said God had anointed my hands and that it was okay. After that day, my grandmother told me, she knew I would be good with my hands.

CHAPTER 6

The Decision

It was the summer before my senior year and it was time for AAU Nationals in Chattanooga, Tennessee. It was going to be the last time I would be able to showcase my talent to schools and coaches. Every time I played, the stands were packed with coaches trying to get a last look at me. During that time I also met players who put a good word in for the schools they attended. Malikah would even call and tell me I should consider Iowa, where she had chosen to play. Letters would be left by various colleges at the hotels where my team and I stayed, to try and sway me towards their schools. Sometimes coaches would even show up at my hotel. Whatever a coach could legally do to gain a recruiting advantage over their competitors, they would. My teammates called the reactions of the college coaches "The Glare." This was when I would walk onto the court and every coach would try to make eye contact with me. They would stare at me for a few seconds until I looked at them, they would then give me "The Glare." We would just laugh as we warmed up and prepared to play.

Following AAU Nationals I began to prepare for the start of my senior year. This year marked the end of my days playing with the guys. The boys had started to physically develop and it was too hard on my body trying to keep up with them. However, I would still head up to DS Park in Ravenswood and watch them play in the PAL tournament. While I was at a game I ran into Lamar Odom, who had just completed his freshman year at CTK. We talked about our summers and what we expected of our seasons to come at CTK. We had become friends because I used to practice with his team after the season was over. Lamar and I would play one-on-one all the time. He was 6'2 as a freshman, but less than 3 months later; he stood in front of me at nearly 6'7. The day I saw him he was sitting on the bench, not playing. So, I asked him why. He said his knees were bothering him because he had grown so much over the summer. I guess that's what happens when you grow that fast. During those last days of summer I would chat with all the guys I knew and watch games, while trying to find new moves to work on.

Soon school was back in session and I couldn't believe it was already my senior year. Everything seemed to be coming together. My mom was still doing well and my dad had decided that he was going to stay at my grandmother's. He wanted to spend as much time with me as he could before I left to go to college. I was looking forward to the time we'd get to spend together. My parents had finally decided that they were better apart and would try their best to remain friends. My mom had moved on and was already dating someone. It was really hard for me to see my mom with her new boyfriend. Every time I met him it was like the movie *50 First Dates*, as if each encounter was for the first time. I had to warm up to him again and again. I was bitter that she was dating; I wanted her to be together and happy with my father. My grandmother softened my feelings and told me that it was for the best that my parents had grown apart.

Despite my feelings, life still went on, and so did the school year. I remember walking into the gym one day after school and the guys were there having a dunk contest. I was watching Craig "Speedy" Claxton throw down 360 dunks at just 5'9. He had an incredible leaping ability and I loved to watch him go! Next thing I knew, Ira Miller and Eric Barkley, members of the boys' team, were telling me, "Mique, you should try." I got out there and I tried to show my CTK family what I could do. I kept just barely missing each time I tried.

College coaches were now allowed to visit and watch preseason work-outs. My teammates almost went crazy at the sight of so many famous women's basketball coaches. My point guard, Kristeena Alexander (GWU), always had lots of jokes about the situation. I would tell her, "You better work hard so they can see you." During the beginning of the school year I spent a lot of time talking to coaches over the phone. My two favorite coaches to talk to were Mickie DeMoss from the University of Tennessee and Tammi Reiss from the University of Virginia; they were easy to talk to and the conversation flowed naturally. Both would try to get me to tell them just how serious I was in considering them, but that was hard to do without having had a home visit yet.

I wasn't the kid that had grown up going to college games or having a favorite college team my family and I supported. I wasn't that player who knew where she had wanted to go all of her life. This was a completely new experience and I really had to explore all of my options. I wanted to make the best all around decision. So my plan was to have home visits with each of the coaches from the schools I was interested in and then visit the schools where I had not yet been. I decided that I would have Tennessee, UConn, UVA, Purdue, and Penn State come to our home. Mr. Cannizzaro agreed to do the scheduling. Penn State wanted to be the first visit, while Tennessee asked to be my last. Mr. Cannizzaro came to all of my home visits. I lived in a rough neighborhood and he didn't want any of the knuckleheads in my neighborhood to harass any of the coaches.

Mr. C. was a retired NYC Detective and had a license to carry a gun so I knew they would be safe. He played the role of security for my visits, which was very much needed. When you are from the hood no one bothers you, but when you are an outsider coming in, all eyes are on you from the moment you step a foot inside. I remember thinking to myself, "What are these people going to think when they have to ride the elevator that smells like pee?" However, my thoughts were eased when my grandmother asked management to clean the elevator. Otherwise, I would have had them take the stairs up. In the projects there are a flight of stairs between the lobby and the first floor. We lived on the first floor so they wouldn't have had to come far.

When Penn State coach Rene Portland came to visit, I was impressed by her warmth and values. My grandmother really enjoyed the visit, too, and it was overall a positive interaction. Next up was UVA. I had a great relationship with assistant Tammi Reiss. She was the youngest of the coaches, and because of this she was easy to relate to. It also helped that my friend from NYC, Jamal Robinson, was on the men's team at UVA. He said she was considered "good people." With her, I was easily able to drop my guard. Out of all of the coaches, we probably spent the most time talking. She also introduced me to the team manager at the time, Angela O'Neal. Tammi had nicknamed Angela "Sha-nay-nay," after the character on "Martin." I felt we could joke around and talk about almost anything. I expressed how my grandmother wanted me to attend a school where the coaches pushed the players towards excellence all the way around, both on and off the court. Angela then said, "Look, what I'm about to tell you may sound crazy, but if I were you, I would go to Tennessee."

My jaw dropped as I listened to her words. I could not believe that the manager for the University of Virginia team was telling me this. She assured me that I would be more successful at Tennessee than I would at UVA. She said that coach Summitt and her staff were the best in the business and that they graduated their players. I was at a loss for words. No one had been this honest with me through this whole process. I thought that Debbie Ryan was very nice and my grandmother loved what the school stood for academically, but what Angela had just told me impacted me in a strong way. I had grown to trust her and trusted she wouldn't lead me in the wrong direction, even though she doing something as crazy as endorsing her competition. I quietly contemplated her words as I continued my visits.

Geno Auriemma and Chris Dailey made the visit from UConn. What I loved about the visit with them was how matter-of-fact Geno was. My grandmother felt that they didn't talk enough about academics, but I disagreed. I felt he had confidence in his program and in his players. He made it clear that his goal was for his players to leave UConn being the best people and best basketball players that they could be, and it was up to the player to take full advantage of their opportunities academically.

Next up would be the Purdue visit. This would be my most embarrassing visit for more than one reason. First, my grandmother dozed off as they went into the details about the school and the program. I thought Coach Dunn was very witty. She and her assistant at the time, MaChelle Joseph, had Coach C. and me laughing. They had a huge sense of humor, but were still very thorough and to the point.

As everyone was just starting to forget about my grandmother dozing off on them, the phone rang. I quickly ran to answer; it was Angela O'Neal on the other end. She said that she was in Queens and wanted to swing by the house. I told her that would be okay but that I was finishing up with my Purdue visit. Soon after I hung up the phone there was a knock at my door and it was Angela. She had arrived much quicker than I anticipated. I thought the coaches from Purdue would have been long gone by the time she showed up. Talk about feeling uncomfortable! I saw Coach Dunn's eyes open wide and her mouth drop open. I politely ushered Angela into another room in our apartment and continued with my visit. After that, I feared a NCAA investigation was soon to follow. I liked Coach Dunn but at the end of the day I didn't feel a connection to Indiana. I would be there all by myself without having any family nearby, and that was important to me.

My last visit was with Coach Summitt and Mickie DeMoss from Tennessee. Mickie was funny and easy to talk to. I also enjoyed talking to Coach Summitt, but I was a little intimidated by her. I mostly sat there in awe: I couldn't believe that I had the best coaches in women's basketball in my home! I remember saying, "This is unreal; I have Pat Summitt in my house. You look so fake!" My grandmother gave me the look of death and told me to apologize immediately. I didn't mean that she *literally* looked fake. I was trying to say that it was surreal having Pat Summitt at my home in Astoria, New York. This by far was the best visit. They knocked it out of the park. Some other schools told me that I would start as a freshman on the team or made other promises, but Coach Summitt did none of that. She did, however, look my grandmother in the eye and tell her that she would make sure I graduated. My grandmother was more than pleased to hear her talk about her pride in academics and her 100% graduation rate. She was upfront and honest and I appreciated that.

However, what was most memorable about her visit happened earlier in the day after Coach Summitt watched my team and me practice. She asked me if I wanted to go and get something to eat, and of course, I said yes. So with a hunger growing in my stomach I suggested we go to Burger King. It was down the street from my school and the first thing that popped in my head. When classmates and my teammates found out later that week that I had taken her there, they made fun of me for months. I would hear things like, "Come on! You took Pat Summitt to *Burger King*?" Honestly, I didn't even think anything of it. It was close, convenient, and I went there often with my friends.

Each coach that had visited in my home told me what I could expect playing for them and attending their universities. I was given a detailed description of what life might be like as a student athlete at their schools. I was impressed at how well all the visits went, and now it was time to make a decision on what schools I would go visit. I had family near all the schools I was considering, except for Purdue. Having some type of support system was important to me. When I considered Tennessee I thought about how much of my family was from the south and how my grandmother and Coach Summitt shared their own language as they related to one another. Together they talked about their roots and where they had come from.

After great consideration, I decided not to visit UConn and Purdue. Both of the coaches respected my decision. Coach Dunn told me that if I wasn't going to Indiana, that I better sign with the school with the orange. UConn, on the other hand, was *too* close to home. I needed to

CHAPTER 6: The Decision

get away from my immediate family and grow up. I knew that if I were that close to home I'd find myself distracted by friends and family too often. I also wanted more of a challenge. UConn destroyed every team that they played in the Big East Conference. I really wanted to like Purdue, but I didn't know a single person at the university and I would be all alone. With all of these factors in mind I decided to visit Penn State first and Tennessee next, followed by the University of Virginia.

When visiting a school, they normally elect an upper classman or two to host the recruit. My hostesses at Penn State were Kim Calhoun and Tina Nicholson. They were the team's star players. I was very excited to meet the girls and get a glimpse into college life. They took me around and showed me the athletic facilities. I stayed in the dorms during my trip. Penn State was known for their football team and legendary coach Joe Paterno. When we drove around the campus there was something football related everywhere. The campus and town certainly had a team spirit.

When I arrived, I went to the basketball office to meet up with all of the coaches where they refreshed me about their program. Afterwards, Kim came and got me and we headed to meet the team. We ate dinner, hung out at the dorms, and later on that night we went to a frat party. It was pretty cool to see college from this perspective. They did their best to show me what it was going to be like as a college student here. That night we ran into Penn State's men's basketball star, John Amaechi, who was really nice. For dinner we met at Coach Portland's home, where I had the opportunity to meet her family and the rest of the team. Everyone went around and introduced themselves. I heard all sorts of stories about why the women chose Penn State. One girl had been a fan of the program since she was young, while others wanted to stay within the state and be close to home. Some came because of Coach Portland. Coach Portland herself assured me that I would never feel alone or lost. The next day she and I went to a volleyball game together and when it was over she took me to the airport. I had an awesome visit and could see myself as a Nittany Lion.

As soon as I arrived back home, my grandmother had a million questions. Of course, the very first thing that popped out of her mouth was, "Was the school too big for you?" I told her that it wasn't, and that being from NYC, I was used to a lot going on. This made her laugh. Later that night I spoke with Tennessee assistant, Mickie DeMoss, about my Penn State Visit. She had asked me if I had a great time and I told her yes. I don't know what prompted me to do this, but during that conversation I told Mickie, "Look, I'm coming to Tennessee if my grandmother likes the school and the people." I told her that my grandmother was a good judge of character and that I trusted her opinion.

As the process went on I learned that when recruiting, some coaches liked to use things against others in order to gain an advantage. I had started hearing a lot of rumors about Coach Summitt's sexual preference. As a sheltered 17-year-old, that prompted me to ask Assistant Coach Mickie DeMoss if Coach Summitt was bisexual. As it came out of my mouth I really had no idea what I had just asked. Honestly, it didn't really matter to me. At the end of the day I wanted to play for the coach that could get the best out of me. Mickie said, "Chamique, I don't know what Pat does. I know that she is married and has a son. That's her business, and really, Chamique, does it matter?" I said no and that was the end of that conversation.

Soon thereafter, I was off to the University of Tennessee for my second visit. This time however, my grandmother decided to come along. I had Penn State on my mind, but I had to clear it and refocus. As we approached Knoxville by plane all I could see were big cornfields and cows. I remember thinking to myself, "Where are we going? Have I made a horrible decision?" I arrived on a Friday, so Coach Summitt just wanted to show us the locker room and take me to the campus to meet up with Tiffani Johnson, who would be my host. She took my grandmother to dinner and back to the hotel. Tiffani and I had become friends over the AAU circuit, so I felt comfortable with her. She showed me around the dorms and took me to the strip where all the college students hung out. She said, "Mique, you have to sign here. We could do some great things." I asked her if the coaches had changed at all since her committing to them and she said no. Mickie, who recruited both of us, was apparently just as silly as ever and really helped her to adjust. She went on to say that Pat was Pat and she would always make sure I did what I was supposed to do. As Tiffani talked I thought to myself, "They sound like good cop, bad cop."

Mickie certainly did have a great sense of humor, which made it easy to connect with her. One time, she had me call her good friend, Carolyn Ross, during my recruiting to tell her I wanted to come to Florida as a prank. She listened as she heard the words flow from my mouth, only to find out seconds later that it had all been a horrible joke. I knew that if nothing else happened as I thought it would I would at least get to laugh with Mickie and my teammates.

That Saturday they took me for breakfast, then took my grandmother and me to meet the Athletic Director, Joan Cronan, the academic team, and sports staff. We had a really busy morning, but everyone was so pleasant. Later that night we met at Coach Summitt's home for dinner with the rest of the team and staff. Her home was on a lake and was beautiful, but even more impressive was her cooking. She had a full spread chicken, steak, green beans, corn casserole, salad and these amazing rolls. My eyes were so big and I dove into her food as if I had not eaten in weeks. Even my grandmother spoke highly of it. That evening, Coach Summitt asked me if I could see Knoxville, Tennessee in my future. I just smiled, but in my head I was saying, "Heck, yes!"

After dinner I went back to the dorm and spent time with Tiffani for the rest of the night. She asked me over and over if I was coming. I told her again and again that I just wasn't sure and that I really didn't know. I just wanted to make a good decision. One thing I did love about Tennessee was that color orange. Boy, was it everywhere and it kept me alert, to say the least. I remember thinking to myself as I fell asleep in her dorm room, "This feels right." I then asked God for direction. I was torn. All I could think about was being a Lady Vol and making my grandmother happy as I drifted to sleep.

That Sunday we went and had lunch at Gibbs Hall, the football dorm.

I had a meeting with the girls' team in the locker room. It still plays in my mind like it was yesterday. The girls said to me that they really enjoyed getting to know me, but they wanted to know what my decision was going to be. I said that I had appreciated everything, especially the hospitality, but that I would be going to the University of Virginia. Man! They looked at me like I was crazy. Mickie's sense of humor must have rubbed off on me. After a few seconds passed I said, "Hey! I'm just kidding. I'm coming to UT!" I asked them not to say anything because I wanted my grandmother and the coaches to hear it from me first. During my final meeting with Coach Summitt, I told her that I was coming to the University of Tennessee to be a Lady Vol. She hugged me and was so excited. I also asked her not to mention it to my grandmother. I had something special for Grandma June up my sleeve.

I felt really good about my future and I was filled with excitement. Now, it was time to pull the prank of the year on my grandmother. While we were on the plane back to NY she had asked me how I liked it. I completely downplayed it by saying that it was just okay. She said she really enjoyed herself and loved the people. She went on to say how comfortable she felt that the coach would provide me with structure and help me to stay on track. She emphasized how she wanted me to have my college degree in four years. I looked her into her eyes and said, "Grandma, I'm going to the University of Virginia." She replied, "Over my dead body!" She got really upset and snappy. I told her to relax and that it was my decision. I told her that she had to accept it. She was so angry with me that I soon blurted out, "I'm just joking!" I told her that my choice was actually Tennessee and she smiled and started to cry. She assured me that I was making the right choice.

The next day I headed to school and met up with Mr. C to tell him about my final plans. He asked me if I was sure and I confidently said yes. He said, "Chamique, I have watched you grow into a fine young woman. I support you and wish you all the best." He did tell me however, how I would have to call the other coaches myself and tell them of my decision.

He said that doing so was a part of growing up. When I spoke to UVA Assistant Tammi Reiss she was disappointed, but wished me the best in my career. She did ask me why UVA did not make the cut and I told her honestly, that it was because I knew too many girls on the team. I think that going there would have been the easy thing to do. I had realized that I couldn't pick a college just because my friends were there. She said that she understood and respected that.

The call that I dreaded making was to Coach Portland, because I sincerely liked Penn State. I called and got no answer, so I left a message asking her to return my call. When she did, I just cut to the chase and said, "Coach, I committed to Tennessee on my visit." I told her I was really sorry and that I wished her and her program the best. She wished me luck as well and then we hung up. It was about an hour later when the phone rang. I answered only to find that Coach Portland on the other end asking me to reconsider. She personally thought that I was making a mistake. I told her that I felt confident with my decision, but thanked her once again. I couldn't believe that she had called me back and said that I was making the wrong decision. I guess that was all a part of the emotions that come with losing out on a great player.

On the first day we could sign, the other seniors and I had a signing day press conference. It was there that I announced I would be accepting an athletic scholarship to the University of Tennessee at Knoxville. I could have not been happier that day. They had a celebration with cake, ice cream and balloons for us. I couldn't believe I would be heading to college next year, and that high school was almost over. I was thankful that I had still had some time left to spend with my family and friends and had a season to play. I couldn't help but reflect on how far I had come.

That same night I went home and cried my eyes out thinking about how good God had been to me. He had brought me so far, further than I could have ever dreamed for myself. I asked him to keep me safe and to surround me with good people. I used to wake up in the middle of the night and I would see the light on in the living room. When I would peek through the door, I would see my grandmother down on her knees praying. I didn't know what her conversation with God was about, but I knew I was one of her blessings, as she was one of mine.

Just as any other season, CTK went through our ups and down, but we stuck it out as a team. Now that I had committed to Tennessee I was able to relax and enjoy my senior year. It was great that my dad was living with us because we got to do things as we had prior to my parent's alcoholism. I was more independent now, and growing into a young woman, and my dad would always make sure that my focus was on schoolwork and basketball. He didn't want me to unintentionally mess up my opportunity by slacking off or taking things for granted. I would giggle to myself whenever he brought up boys. He made sure I knew that I should always be treated with consideration and respect.

We would go to the courts and shoot, talk, and play one-on-one. He was pretty bad so I would usually win. Now that I lived with him I had a greater understanding of who he was. I knew my dad was a drinker, but I never saw him being as bad as my mom. He was never abusive. He was a social drinker who liked to listen to music before falling asleep. Sometimes when my dad drank he would talk to himself. I would often catch him staring into space having a full conversation about what I considered to be nothing. I thought nothing of it and just blamed it on the alcohol. I was just happy to have him there.

Since my dad was staying with us, that meant that he could pick me up from late basketball practice and I didn't have to ride the bus. I would no longer have to wait in the cold for the bus or fall asleep as I rode home. I was really excited and happy to see him after practice, until he started showing up drunk. Like when I was a child, I had to bang on the car window for his attention because he would be sleeping with the music blasting. It only happened a few times to start, but then it started happening more frequently. So I eventually asked him to teach me how to drive so that I could get us home safely. He gladly accepted and taught me how to drive in an empty lot one day in Astoria. I learned quickly and was soon behind the wheel driving us home. I never told my grandmother because I didn't want her to worry or hear a lecture about his lack of responsibility. So whenever my father would pick me up drunk I would just tell him to let me drive. I would always take the back way home when I drove. Without a driver's license I didn't want to risk us getting caught. The drive would take about 30 minutes, but we would be safe.

I realized that whatever was happening with my dad was happening more often. Even when he wasn't drinking I would catch him talking to himself. He would have episodes when he would just stare into space, and it was starting to scare me. I would ask him if he was okay and he would say that he was fine. I didn't want to bother him, but in the back of my mind I knew something wasn't right. I even got up the courage to talk to my grandmother about it, but she also said he was all right. She figured he was probably just stressed and this was his way of coping with it. But stressed or not, when is it okay to talk to yourself and blurt out random things when other people are around? I shrugged it off and focused on finishing my senior year.

I was about to cap off a storybook career at CTK, but I soon learned that not all stories have a happy ending. After a game one night I waited as I always did for my father or uncle to come and pick me up. My Uncle George was supposed to pick me up this particular night, but he never showed. I waited, waited and waited until I was the only one left standing outside of the gym. I began to worry because however flaky my family could be, I had never waited this long. As I started to walk towards the payphone to call home I saw Mr. C's car coming back down the hill. He parked his car and walked toward me. I told him that I was still waiting for my family to come and get me. He looked up and I knew that what ever he was going to say next wasn't going to be good. My heart raced and I first asked if something had happened to my grandmother. He said, "No, your grandmother is fine, but they called me and asked if I would take you home."

A million thoughts ran through my head as we drove. I had no idea what was going on. I felt like we hit every red light as we drove that night.

We just couldn't get there fast enough. As we approached my block, Mr. C told me that he loved me and that if I needed anything that I could call him. I said okay and thanked him. When the car finally stopped in front of my house I ran as fast as I could to the apartment.

When I opened the door my whole family was there. My eyes searched for my grandmother; I needed to see that she was okay. I then looked through the room and saw my mom, brother and aunt, so I knew my immediate family was alive. There was a picture in the middle of the table that everyone was circled around so I got closer to see what they were looking at. As I approached the table, my Aunt Hattie said that Uncle TJ, my hero, had been in a bad accident and had died.

My thoughts went to his family in Montana. His children were young and would now have to grow up without their father. My heart was broken. He was my measuring stick as far as basketball was concerned. He had taught how to play the game. He was the only person in my family who had traveled the road I was heading down. Even though he didn't live in New York, he was the glue that kept out family whole. I know it was hardest for my grandmother, but she tried her best to hide it. I wanted to take away her hurt as she had done so often for me, but I didn't know how. There is nothing that could ever make up for the loss of her youngest child.

Not knowing how she was really doing killed me, so I decided it might be best for me to read my grandmother's journal. I just wanted to know how she really felt and what I could do to ease her pain. I read each page, hoping to find a remedy for her sorrow. She wrote about how she didn't know how she got to and from work every day because her mind was consumed with thoughts of TJ. She wrote that there had been nothing worse in the world than losing her child. He words cried off of the pages but I realized once again that she was the strongest person I had known and in time she would heal.

I stayed home while my family went to Montana for the funeral. I didn't want to go because I wanted to celebrate my uncle as I had remembered him, as loving and full of life. In the back of my head it seemed less real if I didn't go. Going to my high school prom didn't feel right either, so I stayed home alone and reflected on what he meant to me. With the death of my uncle I quickly learned that no matter what happens, no matter how bad, time stops for no one. I had to pull myself together and move past this tragedy. So I focused on winning another state championship. Each time I played I gave the game all of who I was. I now knew what a gift life was and I wanted to experience mine to the fullest. We were once again champions, winning our 4th straight title. We were ranked in the USA Today Top 25 high school poll. I was named an All-American and won pretty much every Player of the Year honor in New York and nationwide. Every award dinner and every speech I gave, I always made sure to thank my uncle for inspiring me. Without him I may have never been able to live my dream of playing college basketball on a big stage.

THIRD
QUARTER

CHAPTER 7

The Rude Awakening

I was increasingly excited to be heading to Knoxville to start college. The summer before I was to start school, I was sent a summer workout plan by the UT staff. Rain or shine, I was on it diligently. I would get strange glances from people as I ran through my neighborhood doing my workouts. I was determined to be in great shape by the time I got to college.

In anticipation of my freshman year away, I asked my family for $2,000. I had always worn uniforms to schools or was in athletic gear for ball so my wardrobe was seriously lacking. I mean, I couldn't show up in my high school uniform on the first day of classes. At first my family thought I was crazy, but after I pleaded my case they awarded me the money. Just before I left for school I met my mom downtown to get the money from her. She had won $1500 on a scratch-off lottery ticket. I met her and we took it and cashed it in. I thought my mom was so lucky; no one in my family had ever won anything like that. She also wanted to buy me something for school. I told her I really wanted was a stereo for my dorm room. We spent that day together shopping. It was a rare and special moment and we both had a good time. I was happy I had gotten a stereo and some new clothes, but I was more excited about the mom-and-daughter time we were spending. Our relationship was deeply fractured, but this day together marked the moment when we both began to heal.

As I was packing and getting my stuff together for school, I sat on my bed and looked at all the posters on my wall: Jordan, Magic, Teresa Edwards, and college stars like Othella Harrington and Jason Kidd. Each of them had been a great inspiration to me and I hoped to leave my mark as they had all done. While packing I also looked over my old journals. I used to write a lot as a kid because it helped me to deal with the stresses of my parents, among other things. One young entry written years ago read that I would be the first girl to play in the NBA. I had big aspirations and dreams and was determined to fulfill them all.

My Aunt Anita and Uncle George had decided that they would take me to college. I was flooded with emotion as I prepared to leave my small three bedroom apartment and the courts that made me into one of the best young players in the nation. I was also leaving the woman who had nurtured me and who showed me that anything is possible. As I thought about these things my eyes filled with tears. Before I left that day, my grandmother sat me down and said, "Chamique, you know right from wrong. Please continue to remain humble and don't forget to thank God for all your blessings." I hugged her tightly and told her that I loved her.

Once I was on that plane headed to Knoxville, I kept thinking to myself how surreal it was. The bright lights of New York City were gone. This cow-studded landscape was where I would be spending the next four years of my life. When I arrived at my dorm my roommate, Kim Smallwood, was already there with her mom, Laura Newsome. At first sight Kim was physically imposing. She had muscles in places I didn't know muscles grew. In all of my years of playing sports I had never seen a girl built like this. Kim was a hurdler for UT's track team. She loved and excelled at track, but also loved basketball. While being recruited by UT she mentioned this, so the coaches were able to work it out and let her play both sports. Her mother and my aunt and uncle connected with each other right away. All of us sat there in the room and thought about what we needed in order to make our space feel more like home. We decided on the things we needed, went to the store together, and then had dinner. When we got back from dinner we found out that we shared a suite with two of our teammates, Kellie Jolly and Misty Greene. They were both from great high school programs and they were two of the top players in the state of Tennessee. Kellie was a point guard and Misty was a three point specialist. As we exchanged words for the first time it sounded like they were speaking another language. I really had to get used to their southern twangs. They also had to get used to the way I talked. I was a fast-talking, slang-using New Yorker. Between the four of us, there was a great mix of personalities. Even though we came from different backgrounds, we got along wonderfully once I warmed up to them, I was probably the most talkative and energetic of the group. I always wanted to be out and about doing something. Kellie was really laid back and the most mature, Misty was fun and loved to socialize, and Kim was really shy. However, once she came out of her shell, she was quite entertaining.

I will never forget the first meeting we had as a team. Pat and her staff welcomed us and stressed the importance of us being responsible, being on time, and being respectful of others. They then handed us binders and said that everything we planned to do would need to go in it. Coach Summitt stressed the importance of being well organized and how it would carry over into everything that we did. Yes, we were there on athletic scholarships, but we were students first and she was going to make sure that we left her program better women with degrees. She then went to the board and started to ask us questions about respect and discipline. Long before we knew it, we had an outline to follow, "The Tennessee Definite Dozen." Coach Summitt had created this list over her years at Tennessee:

1. Respect Yourself and Others.
2. Take Full Responsibility.
3. Develop and Demonstrate Loyalty
4. Learn to Be a Great Communicator.
5. Discipline Yourself So No One Else Has To
6. Make Hard Work Your Passion.
7. Don't Just Work Hard, Work Smart.

8. Put the Team before Yourself
9. Make Winning an Attitude.
10. Be a Competitor
11. Change Is a Must
12. Handle Success Like You Handle Failure

I walked out of that meeting more than a little overwhelmed. I came into the locker room with not even a pen, and left with a platform, rather a blueprint, for success. That binder was the first tool given to me to help achieve my adult goals.

The first week of school left me exhausted. I ran around campus registering for classes while trying to get acclimated to my new home. I had no idea what I wanted to major in, but I knew I liked math, so in the back of my head I figured something in finance. Before making a decision, I wanted to get through the first year of school to see if that was what I was truly interested in.

My roommates and I had attended a few freshman mixers and other campus gatherings. Tiffani Johnson, who was now a sophomore on the team, introduced me to several students. At a meeting for all the freshman athletes, I made some friends and exchanged contact information. In those days we didn't have cell phones, so we would pass on our dorm room telephone number and the name of the dorm building just in case anyone wanted to meet up. During my freshman year I lived in an all-girls dorm that had really strict rules. Our guests had to leave by 11 p.m. or we would get written up. Once written up, you couldn't have visitors for a certain period of time.

I really liked Torrey, another freshman and a member of the men's basketball team. He was tall and athletic and he had a good sense of humor. We hung out all the time from August to November. We had a lot in common and enjoyed each other's company. I will never forget the day he told me that he wanted to see other people. My jaw dropped and I felt a sharp pain; this was the first time something like this had ever happened to me.

However, I didn't feel bad for long. He had broken up with me because I didn't want to have sex with him. I was still a virgin and I was not ready to take that step yet. I didn't need to be with anyone who didn't respect that anyway. Initially, it was weird seeing him around campus, but I got over it quickly. I was proud to be a virgin. Just because everyone was having sex, that didn't mean that I had to. I hadn't dated much during high school, even though lots of guys liked me. My head was always in sports and that was my focus. I was more like a tomboy and proud of it. It wasn't even until high school that I started developing friendships with girls. Before that, I had always just been "one of the guys." My best friends growing up had mostly been boys.

Soon preseason started for basketball and I was in for a rude awakening. As a team we would have 5:30 a.m. runs before class. I had never been much of a morning person so it took some time getting used to. Muscles that I didn't even know I had started to ache. Basketball workouts were so intense, like nothing I had gone through in high school. This was a serious wake-up call and I soon felt like I had never picked up a ball before. For me, it wasn't as bad physically as it was mentally. As soon as I stepped onto the court all I would hear was the sound of Coach Summitt's voice. I seemed like she yelled my name as loud as she could each time she said it: "Holdsclaw, rebound," "Holdsclaw, run the floor harder," "Holdsclaw, box out." There were days where I wasn't sure if I would make it.

Classes were in full swing too, and they were just as demanding. Our 5:30 a.m. runs were catching up with me. It became harder and harder for me to stay awake in my 8 a.m. English class. Coach Summitt had a rule that players must sit within the first three rows of the class, so it was obvious whenever I fell asleep. My English professor didn't take it easy on me either. He would say things like, "Looks like someone isn't sleeping at night," and would slam a book shut to wake me up. I would jump out of my seat in embarrassment each time he did it. Frustrated and exhausted, I decided to drop his class and take English later in the year.

Academically, I was struggling, but I knew it was because I had a lot going on. I was doing my best to find balance in my new life. I would be in study hall joking around, bored to death, and unable to focus. There were a thousand other places I wanted to be during those two hours. Soon reports and grades from my professors started coming in and there was nothing positive about either. So Coach Summitt and our academic advisor, Kerry Howland, sat me down and had a talk. Kerry wanted to make sure I knew I had resources that could help me and that tutors were available whenever I needed them. I needed goods grades in order to play and no one wanted to risk me becoming ineligible. I knew I had to make a change and commit more time and effort to my studies.

And boy was I mistaken if I thought preseason had been tough! It was a walk in the park compared to what we did during official practice. It was far more demanding than any other practice I had been through. The only thing that was reassuring was that games would start soon and we would have to practice less. Blood, sweat and tears were shed each practice and if it wasn't good enough, we went harder and longer. I remember worrying that Coach Summitt might have a split personality. She would be tough as nails on the court, but once we left she wanted to laugh and give hugs. I didn't get it and was too exhausted and drained to try. I wanted to work hard and be successful, but I wasn't sure if this is what I had signed up for. I would dramatically joke in the locker room that if she made us run like this again someone should fake passing out so that practice could be canceled. I tried my best to figure out a way to get us out of running so much. It didn't matter where I was on campus, I could always hear her voice in my head: *Chamique, Chamique, Chamique, box out, rebound.* When I didn't do enough, she would put everyone on the line. She told me that I had the potential to be a great rebounder and she was going to pull it out of me one way or the other. She said, "Mique, you have to exert effort and go get it." I would roll my eyes as I walked to the line frustrated. Two of our seniors, Michelle Marciniak and Latina Davis, were annoyed that I was the cause for all the extra running. All I heard was deep sighs as we placed our feet on the line to run. I started to feel discouraged and as though I could not do anything right. It was our junior forward, Abby Conklin, a sharp shooting player from Indiana, who lifted me up with some words of wisdom. She said, "*You* may think you are doing things right, but Coach Summitt wants it done her way." She told me not to worry and that all the first year players go through a transitional period. Abby renewed my confidence that day.

After practice, I went over to talk to Coach. I confidently said, "Look, please stop making everyone run for me. I will run by myself, my teammates are getting upset with me." Not sure what her response would be I held my breath. Coach agreed and I exhaled a sigh of relief. I knew she had only agreed because she knew I had finally gotten it. She had broken me down and built me back up. My lesson was learned. I went on to lead the team in rebounding all four of my years there, and I became Tennessee's all-time leader in rebounds in both men's and women's basketball.

I won myself a starting role as a freshman, and my teammates were gaining more and more confidence in me. For one of our preseason games that year we had an exhibition game against our U.S. national team. The team boasted stars like Lisa Leslie, Sheryl Swoopes, Katrina McClain, Dawn Staley, and Teresa Edwards. I was playing against women I looked up to and respected. I was excited for the challenge. I played well that game, scoring 19 points and I soon became a fan favorite that everyone was talking about. After that I went to the gym each day inspired to be better.

The first semester grades were in and all I was able to scrape together a 2.5 GPA. I knew I was in the doghouse. My grandmother had made it very clear to me that she didn't want to see anything less than a 3.0. On top of that, Pat and her staff were always on me about my grades. I knew I would get a lecture, but it didn't go as bad as I thought it would. I had my guard up and ready for whatever blow was coming my way. However, both my grandmother and Coach understood that I was going through a big adjustment and that it would take more time before I was fully acclimated. I needed to shift my focus off just basketball and really hit the books. I knew I hadn't applied myself and could do much better.

There were other struggles I would encounter during that first year. There were times when Coach Summitt and I would bump heads. She would just yell at me, which infuriated me. I'm not the type of person you have to yell at. Everyone is motivated differently and that technique didn't work with me at all. I was used to my high school coach, Mr. Mackey, who had gotten on my case a lot. But how he got on my case and how she got on my case differed so greatly that I didn't know how to deal with it.

One time, Coach Summitt kicked me out of practice because she said I didn't want to practice hard enough. I said that wasn't the case. She responded and asked me what my problem was. I told her that I was just tired as I rolled my eyes at her. She looked at me square in the face and kicked me out. I was angry beyond measure. I felt like I was always under the microscope. Everything I did was criticized and watched and I had reached a breaking point. Every ounce of desire to play had been drained from me. I thought for sure that I was going to transfer.

I went as far as calling my grandmother and telling her of my plans. She said, "No Chamique. You are going to stay right there and work through this." My grandmother went on to tell me that Pat had beat me to the punch and called her, warning her that my grandmother could probably expect a call from me wanting to transfer. Coach was always a step ahead and grew to know me well. After talking to my grandmother, Mickie DeMoss played mediator while Coach Summitt and I sat down and talked. She told me that she knew she asked a lot of me as a freshman, but it was because she believed in me and knew I could do it. She saw potential in me and that's why she was so hard on me. During that meeting I told her how I hated to be yelled at all the time. Up until that point I didn't know how to communicate with her. I expected her to know what I was thinking without ever saying a word, and that was unfair on my part. If we hadn't talked and faced this head on, I probably would have made a life changing mistake and transferred. Simple communication was key, I learned that day.

I played a submissive role my first year and I hid behind being a freshman a lot. There were games where I knew I could have been dominating, but instead I just played my freshman role and did what was expected of me. This went until midseason in a game against Vanderbilt. We found ourselves in battle. They were playing better overall and it showed. Their All American guard Sheri Sam led them at every aspect of the game. This was a big SEC rival with them just down the way in Nashville. The state was only big enough for one of us. I'm not even sure what came over me or gave me the courage to do what happened next.

During a time out, I approached Coach Summitt, tapped her on her shoulder, looked her in the eyes and said, "Coach get me the ball." She did and I made play after play to help us win the game. I've since heard her speak about this moment and even write about it. We both agreed that this was my official welcome to Knoxville. She had never had a player, especially a freshman approach her in that manner. My win-at-all-costs attitude kicked in that day and neither of us ever looked back. From that point on I came through in the clutch.

With the SEC tournament approaching, we were starting a new season. In my head, I always broke down the season into three periods and this was the second. As always, the SEC was very competitive and on any given night, any team could win. My grandmother had decided to come down to watch and I was ecstatic that she would be there to support me. I wanted to play my best, but unfortunately my play was halted when I had injured my knee.

We were lined up on the line as my teammates shot free throws in a game against the University of Alabama when it happened. After a miss by my teammate, one of their players crashed into my knee. I fell to the ground and grabbed my knee as I rolled around in pain. Our trainer, Jenny Moshak, stormed the floor and took me into the back where the doctors examined me. After running a few physical tests they confirmed it was not an ACL rupture, but said I would have to wait to get back to Knoxville to have an MRI after the tournament. My grandmother prayed over my knee and the doctors assured me that everything would be okay. Once we got back to Knoxville, I had an MRI that revealed a second-degree sprain of my MCL. This made playing for the postseason questionable.

With the NCAA tournament approaching everyone was wondering if I would be back or not. I had worked too hard and been through so much just to see it all slip away. I was more than determined not to have my season end this way. I rehabbed my knee hard with our team's trainer and made progress everyday. I was still in a lot of pain. Soon it was a week before our first game and Coach Summitt called me into her office. I walked in and she said that someone had sent a package to me. I opened it up and read the letter that lay on top. It was from Michael Bivins, the founder and member of the groups New Edition and Bell Biv DeVoe. He just wanted to tell me to get healthy and keep up the good work. He had been watching the game when I had gotten injured. You can only imagine how excited I was, but I wasn't able to keep the CDs, T-shirts, and other items he had sent because it was a NCAA violation. So I thanked him for thinking of me and sent them back. The letter was enough, anyway. I was happy he even knew who I was. As a kid, I had loved New Edition and I had their posters all over my walls.

After I settled down, Coach looked at me with her piercing eyes and asked, "Will you be able to play?" I told her, "No." My knee was still weak and I didn't feel stable. I was scared to go back out there too soon and hurt it more. She then told me to think about the many people who cared about me. She pointed out the fact that I would be letting them down. When she said this, I was upset. Tears ran down my face while my blood boiled. I wasn't a quitter and I tried to explain to her that it really did hurt and that it wasn't at 100% yet. As I wiped the tears from my face I had a change of heart. I was going to prove that I wasn't soft and fragile, but strong and resilient. I looked her and told her that I would try. However harsh it may be, she always knew exactly what to say to motivate me.

As I went back to my dorm room, some of the upper classmen called, wanting to see how my meeting went. When they walked in I told them the details and how I was scared to play. They told me that they supported me whether I was able to play or not. One of them said to me, "You are only a freshman and it's only going to get worse for you." I looked at her and said, "I know." They reassured me that it was my decision to make and that they would support me regardless. I thought about it and decided that I would at least try. I didn't want my character questioned or to have my first season end this way.

So I slowly worked my way back into practice that week. We had a high seed in the NCAA tournament so the first couple of games wouldn't be as difficult. I could use it as a tune up to test my knee before we got to the tougher games. Tiffani Johnson was especially excited about the tournament that year because the Final Four was in her hometown of Charlotte, North Carolina. She said to me, "Mique, work hard so we can get me home and we can win a title in front of my family and friends." We were playing so well and moving through our bracket with ease. My knee felt great and we were on our way to Charlotte and the Final Four. I couldn't believe we had come that far, that *I* had come that far.

Coach gave us a speech once we reached the hotel in Charlotte. She wanted our undivided attention. She congratulated us on what we had accomplished so far and told us how proud she was. She then pointed out that we still had work to do if we wanted to leave as champions. She encouraged us to remain focused on what we had sacrificed to be in this position. After that talk I was amped, locked in, and ready to play. I could have gone out and played right then and there. I had never been more inspired. My grandmother and brother came down from New York to support me. It always meant the world to me when they could be there to see me play.

In the semifinal game we had to face our rival, UConn, who had beaten us during the regular season. Still fueled by the hurt we felt at our first loss to them, we made sure we were prepared. This time, we turned the tables on them and played great team basketball. We had a balanced scoring attack with inside-out play. I was still working my way back from my knee injury and finished with just 9 points, but it didn't matter; I was happy we won. Next we would face our SEC rival, Georgia, for the National Championship. Georgia was a good team that was lead by All-American guard, Saudia Roundtree. She was quick and hard to stop. It would take a team effort to slow her down and each of us was up for the challenge.

Coach had a talk with me the night before the championship game to make sure I was staying focused. She assured me that if I remained this way that we would walk away NCAA Champs. I was in such a zone I could barely sleep the night before. When I woke up, I wanted to jump out of bed and start playing immediately. When game time came I could tell that we were ready. Without any fear or doubt we went out there and played one of our best games of the year. We were a well-oiled machine hitting on all cylinders and there was nothing they could do to stop us. We defeated Georgia 83-56. I had 16 points and 14 rebounds. All of our hard work and dedication had paid off. There was never an easy moment that season, but looking back on it I would do it all over again, exactly the same way. The roar from the crowd when we arrived back home to the Knoxville Airport was unbelievable. Our loyal and devoted Tennessee fans were there cheering us on. Tennessee orange took over the place as seas of fans congratulated us. We were like rock stars.

When you play on a team, you learn to sacrifice for the person standing next to you. Pat taught me so much that year. She changed the way I approached the game. There was no work that would be harder than my first year at UT and after surviving that, I felt I was strong enough to accomplish anything. I became mentally tougher that season and really learned how to take the good with the bad. Now I understood it was her job to get the best out of us. Without her ability to finely balance a love-hate relationship we would not have been as successful. It was like I was back in NYC on the courts, trying to prove myself to the guys who overlooked me because I was a girl. All the trash talking that goes on between the lines on the pavement in the hood makes you tougher because you have to defend yourself so hard. The thing was that Pat didn't care for what I had to say. She wanted my actions only, and that meant getting the job done. Thus my first season was very successful. I was a National

Champion and SEC Freshman of the Year. I led my team in scoring (16.2 ppg) and rebounding (9.1 rpg), was named to the All SEC Team, and named a Kodak All-American.

With the season's end it came time for me to solely focus on finishing up the school year strong. I centered my attention on being more organized and bettering my study habits. I wanted to move off campus the following year, but in order to do that, Coach Summitt required a 2.5 GPA. I did my best to study more and stay on top of my work. I spent countless hours in the library. I would study in any quiet place I could find. I worked so hard, but when our grades came in I was disappointed I thought I did better than the 2.5 GPA I received. While I was disappointed, I knew I had met the minimum requirement to be able to move off campus.

Before each of us left for the summer we had an individual meeting with Coach Summitt to discuss our summer plans. I had already decided that I wanted to go home and not attend summer school. I needed a break from schoolwork. I also wanted to participate in a basketball tournament called Olympic Festival. I figured I would play in that and then enjoy my summer with my friends and family.

When we talked Pat expressed how proud she was of my athletic accomplishments. She knew it hadn't been easy. My grandmother always taught me how important it was to look someone in the eyes when they are talking to you, giving them your full attention. But when Pat talked to you and looked at you with her needle eyes, it made it hard to stay focused. However as the conversation went on, her tone started to change. She said, "Mique, you can be just as good of a student as you are a basketball player. You just have to learn to apply yourself and get organized. I know what kind of academic history you have and the high school you come from, so I know that you can do the work. Some people I would accept this from, but not from you. It's just unacceptable." Her tone unmistakably got her point across. Next thing she said was, "Until you get it together, you can't move off campus." I immediately pointed out to her that I'd made the requirement, but she said she didn't care. It was up to her. I was more upset in that instant than I had been all season. Naturally, I caught an attitude and left. I headed back to my dorm room to complain to my teammates. Why was I the one being constantly challenged? I didn't think her decision was fair, but what could I do about it? I decided I couldn't take another minute in Tennessee and was eager to head home for the summer.

As I stepped off the plane I was overwhelmed with joy to be back. I couldn't wait to see my family and friends. I missed the food, the culture, and the low hum of the city. My grandmother was so glad to have me home. All our neighbors came over to see me and asked for autographs. I guess now I was "famous" and everyone knew I had won an NCAA Championship. During my summer stay my grandmother would always make me my favorite meal: pork chops, cabbage, corn pudding, and green beans. She had all my favorite waiting for me warm on the stove when I arrived.

I was happy to see everyone doing well. My grandmother stressed how much she had missed me while I was gone. How the house felt lonely at times without Davon and me there. My mom continued to work at her program and things had started getting serious with a guy she had been dating. My dad seemed to be doing well too. I know he missed me and hated being so far from Davon. I knew it was hard for him to see us being raised by someone else. My father's grandmother had raised him, and although he had a great relationship with her he never wanted his kids to grow up like that. He really wanted to be with his family, but knew that sometimes things don't work out as planned.

I worked tirelessly on getting my parents back together, but that never worked out either. I would set up "chance" meetings between them whenever my mother would come and visit. I often suggested to her that she get back together with my father, but she didn't want to hear it. I had it in my head that it was my mother's fault. I was very bitter toward her for breaking up our family. When my mom tried to introduce me to her new boyfriend I wanted no part of it. When he was around, I was silent. The hopes I had of my family getting back together decreased every time I saw him. I knew I had to let these feelings go. Eventually, I got to the point where I would say hello, but the conversation quickly ended there. I remember when my brother would call me and I would constantly ask him questions about my mother's boyfriend. I wanted to know what he was like and if my mom was happy with him. He would just say that he was nice and that he makes Mom smile. He didn't have a problem with him at all; he loved that she was happy.

Getting back on the court with my boys that summer was a great distraction. Listening to them talk trash and get after me was just like the old days. I was back to my summer routine of hitting the pavement and hooping as much as I possibly could. Now that I had played a year in college everyone wanted to play me one on one to see if I was as good as everyone said. I loved the challenge and it helped keep my skills sharp.

About a month before school started back up I began the track workouts Coach Summitt and her staff had put together for us to prepare for preseason. If I came back from summer break out of shape I knew I would hear about it. I was hoping that this year I would hear my name come out of Coach's mouth far less. So I woke up diligently every morning and got my workout out of the way. I hated running on the track, but if I didn't my life would be hell when I go back to campus. I think it was mental for me. If I had a ball in my hand I would be out there running and playing all day.

It seemed like time was in fast forward that summer and before I knew it was time to leave again. This time around it was hard to leave home. I was really sad to be leaving my grandmother. I wish I could have brought her hugs and home cooked meals to school with me. But I knew how important getting my degree was to her, so I packed my bags.

At that time there was no WNBA, so the best we could do as female players was to travel across the water and establish a career playing overseas. So it was that much more important that I graduate with a degree.

In the back of my mind I always heard my grandmother's speech to me before I went off to college, "Chamique, you are going to graduate in four years and you are *not* coming back here." I understood that and took her words very seriously. I knew that Knoxville was a big part of changing my life, so back to Knoxville I went.

CHAPTER 8

The Cinderella Season

I came back to school more focused than ever. I knew that I would have to step it up in the classroom and be a leader on the court. I had decided that political science was going to be my major. It was something that stimulated me mentally and kept me interested. I was going to start taking those classes right away. I was still upset that I had to live on campus that year, but I took it as a challenge. I wanted to prove to Coach Summitt that I was serious about academics and basketball. I wanted to surpass the expectations she had of me.

We welcomed three new players that season, Kyra Elzy, Niya Butts, and Lashonda Stephens, and we lost Michelle Marciniak and Latina Davis to graduation. They were key players for our team and playing without them was going to be an adjustment, but we had to step up to the challenge if we wanted to defend our title. During our first team meeting, Coach Summitt told the team that HBO would be documenting our season. They wanted to give fans and viewers an inside look at all the ups and downs a championship team goes through. Thus, Coach Summitt asked us to carry ourselves with class because this was something the world would see.

Shortly after I got to school that year I began working on another project: getting my driver's license. I wanted some independence and was tired of asking people to take me places. I wanted to be free to come

93

and go as I pleased. So after passing my road test in Knoxville I called home to my grandmother and dad and asked them for a car. I didn't want anything special, just something to get me from point A to B safely. After some great convincing, my dad agreed to pay $250 a month for a car. I was allowed to pick whatever car I wanted as long as it fit within the budget he gave me.

My teammates and roommates, Tiffani Johnson and Kim Smallwood, helped me look for the perfect car. Kim was also looking for a car so we looked for deals in newspapers and other circulars on campus. We decided to go out to a dealership to see what we could find. We scoped the lot for the perfect cars. We wanted to find something that would give us the most bang for our buck and that didn't scream *Driving Miss Daisy*. After hours of looking we both ended up buying brand new Dodge Neons. I picked a black one and she picked a red one. My car payment was $227 per month. I had gotten what I wanted and came in under budget. I paid my insurance with the extra money I received from the Pell Grant each semester. Other student athletes on campus would call us the 2-for-1 special because of our matching cars.

On one of our many trips out to West Town Mall in our new cars, we met two guys that worked at Foot Locker. Larry and Darryl were students at Knoxville College, small historical black college just minutes away from UT. They were really nice guys and we enjoyed spending time with them. They would keep us up to date on step shows and other things that happened on their campus. They also gave us the inside scoop on when the coolest new shoes were coming out.

But just as we were starting to enjoy our free time, preseason workouts and conditioning started. Jenny Moshak, our long-time trainer at Tennessee, put us through our Tuesday and Thursday 6 a.m. track workouts. This time however, HBO was there, front and center. They certainly got their money's worth! Each day we competed fiercely to make our times. Now that the cameras were on, the assistant coaches would come to watch our workouts. They would try motivate us by telling us to run harder and push through till the end. However, when you are that tired and on the verge of throwing up, you really don't want to hear what anyone has to say.

I will never forget one particular track workout we had to complete. It was 2-400's, 4-200's, 10-100's, and 10-50's. Unfortunately, it was that time of the month and I was suffering badly. I was vomiting and really sick. I had told Jenny that I didn't feel good at all, but she encouraged me to push it out so I didn't have to make it up. In front of HBO's cameras I puked my guts out, horrified and fully exposed for the world to see.

While they were filming, we all hoped that Pat would ease up a little since the cameras were around. Wishful thinking. She was the same ol' Pat. She pushed us and challenged us as she always did. That was the first time I heard her start using the term "mental midgets." It meant not letting that crafty little sucker on your shoulder tell you that you can't do something. She would say, "You just have to bear down and get through." It made for great TV and the cameras loved us.

Everything she said came with purpose. She was getting us ready for what was ahead. We had to replace an all-star backcourt. Junior guard Laurie Milligan and sophomore guard Kellie Jolly battled it out for the point guard position. There were epic battles between them throughout the preseason. They fought to defend each other while running the team and dishing out passes. Kellie was ultimately chosen to lead us at the point. Freshman Kyra Elzy impressed the coaches with her length and defensive abilities. She earned herself as starting position at the 2-spot that season. I was at the small forward, while seniors, Abby Conklin and Pashen Thompson, held down the paint rounding out our starting five.

Kellie was really solid and ran the team to perfection. She didn't have amazing athletic ability, but put deep thought into the game of basketball. The way she approached the game helped me so much. She always knew where to get the ball in order for everyone to be successful. She was a great leader and I trusted her every word. Kellie would go the A through B to C route, but I would figure out how to get to C by bypassing A and B. It may not have been the same route, but we would get there at the same time. I respected the fact she was a true student of the game.

This 1996 to 1997 season proved to be tougher than the first. We just couldn't get in the groove and the pressure was beginning to mount. We didn't understand how our hard work and efforts weren't translating into wins on the court. I was physically and mentally drained because I carried much of the load. We weren't getting that overall production like we had in the previous season. I remember I would be so tired during the games and Kellie would say to me, "Mique, I'm coming to you next play." I would tell her, "Kellie, run it the other way. I'm tired." She would come up to me, grab onto my jersey, look at me and say, "Mique, I'm coming to you, now get open." She would never take no for an answer. We did our best to try and keep things together.

Another player I deeply respected was Abby. She was a sharp shooter from Indiana and her mouth was just as sharp. Her and Coach would bump heads because Abby would say exactly how she felt, while some of us would bite our tongues. It's no coincidence that when Abby left Tennessee she went into coaching. She was always offering her opinion after Coach went over the game plans.

In between games we hosted a highly recruited class of incoming players led by Tamika Catchings, Semeka Randall, Kristin "Ace" Clement, and Teresa Jeter. This would be a big break for us if we could land these players. Coach made sure we knew all we could about them. I was really familiar with Ace since our previous high schools had played against each other every year. Semeka Randall had gone to the same high school as Malikah, my good friend from high school, who transferred to Ohio. Our coaching staff said that these players would help me and the team and I believed them. It took more than just one or two individuals for us to be successful. It would take all of us. I wanted to know what I had to do to get them. I wrote letters, hosted recruits, and spoke with them on the phone when needed. I was devoted to helping us get the best players possible.

I played host to some great people and players during my time at Tennessee. However, the one visit that stands out most was Tamika Catchings, not just because of how talented she was, but because of the person she was. Together we talked about our families and other aspects of our lives. She shared how her parents had divorced and that she lived with her mom in Texas. I told her how my grandmother had raised me and how special that was for me. I asked her if she had watched any of our games. She said no, not many, because the antenna on her television didn't always work. I told her that I was very familiar with that problem. We were having a great conversation when I then asked her, "Why wouldn't you come to TN?" She told me how everyone said we have too many good players and she would not get the same opportunities here as she would at other schools. On the other hand, she wanted to play with the best of the best. I remember smiling and later telling the coaches that Catchings was likely going to commit. She wanted to be a part of something special and we could provide that. We were able to sign the No.1 class that year at Tennessee. All four of those All-Americans committed.

Everyone counted us out that year since we lost ten games early on. We started the season ranked No.4 and had dropped as low as No.11. Our lowest point came when we played the University of Florida in the regular season and lost. I remember looking at the score at the beginning of the game and the score reading Florida 17, Tennessee 1. Nothing went right that day. Instead of being on the same page, we were all on pages in completely different books. Coach was not too happy. After that loss she called us soft and said that we were embarrassing the program. I disagreed. I said I felt that they were a better team than us at this point. Moments after that comment, a clipboard came flying through the air straight for my head. It just barely missed my eye and I was furious. I remember Kyra Elzy and a few other teammates grabbed at me, stopping me from doing or saying something I would later regret. I eventually cooled off. The next day, I met with Pat and we put everything out on the table so we could move past that point. It was the heat of the moment, I was upset and I knew Coach would never intentionally try to hurt one of her players. I was confused because throwing a clipboard at someone's face was never really her style. She said, "Holdsclaw, we have to get fired up and compete because it's not over until the fat lady sings." I agreed and we moved on. We both wanted the same thing.

Our freshman, Kyra Elzy, had started to hit the dreaded freshman wall and her energy was fading fast. Coach told her how much we needed her and that we couldn't afford for her to check out on us. She was our defensive captain. She anchored the defense and had to be vocal, but at the same time she was a gentle, sweet kid. Outside of the court you would never catch her raising her voice. So Coach made a change and started playing Niya Butts a little more. She was a raw offensive player, but an athlete that could lock down defensively. As the season went on, her and Kyra started to complement each other as heads of our defense.

Back in the dorms I started to notice a change in Kim. She was getting less social with us, and she was always on the phone with her godchild. I was confused because I had not heard her speak of this eight-year-old boy ever. I just brushed it off. She then started getting these phone calls from a woman who sounded very professional. She would call several times a day. Every chance she got, it felt like Kim was on the phone. I finally asked her about it and she said it was a good friend of hers who was an attorney in Houston. I didn't really think anything of it. I would even answer the phone and greet the mysterious lady on a first name basis. That was until one day Kim said the woman wanted to speak with me. I thought, "For what?"

When the lady called she explained to me how she was an attorney at a big firm in Houston. She went on to say that she had talked to her boss, and that he said to give me whatever I needed. I was so confused. Why was this total stranger offering to take care of me? She said that they could give me money while in college as long as I promised to let them represent me after college. I told her, "No thank you," and that I couldn't take money from anyone. I said that I thought the conversation was inappropriate. How had Kim become involved with such a person?

We had been given the speech about how we should never accept any gifts or money from anyone outside of our family.

All I could think about was my family telling me not to take a dime from anyone. If I needed something I was to go straight to them. So many thoughts were rolling through my head. Was this person really Kim's friend or was she trying to get me as a client? Finally, I approached Kim about it. She denied it, saying they were long time family friends. All I knew was that it didn't sit right with me. We had lived in a small dorm room together, but now I felt like she was a stranger. In a dorm no conversation is really private and I could hear every phone call she had. I had never heard her mention this woman's name before.

I called home and told my grandmother about what was going on. She said, "Chamique, my number is unlisted and people call here all the time. They all talk about representing you and how they could move me out of the projects now. I tell them politely no thank you." I was shocked. I had no clue what was going on, but I listened to my grandmother's words and strict directions. She said, "Chamique, most people don't give you things for free and most people want something in return. Just remember that. You have a bright future. Just take care of those books and graduate from college. Listen to your coaches and you will be fine." Soon thereafter, I went to talk with Mickie and ended up telling her and Coach Summitt what had occurred. They told me that I did the right thing, and I wondered if they had ever dealt with this type of situation before. This was all new to me, but now that it had happened I would be better prepared should it ever happen again.

When it came to bills, normally my dad would send my car payment two weeks in advance. So it was strange when the payment was due and I had not received payment in the mail. My grandmother said, "Don't worry Chamique. I will just send it to you." I kept trying to reach my dad, but no answer. I left messages, but he didn't call back. I began to worry. I didn't want to stress too much, since it always affected the way I played.

We were getting ready for the SEC Tournament when I received a phone call from my grandmother telling me that a few days prior my dad had been found walking alongside the highway. My heart skipped a beat and I began to think the worst. He was then checked into Creedmore Psychiatric Center. She told me that he had been missing for a month until they finally found him. He had a nervous breakdown and mentally he was no longer the same person. She told me not to worry and that he was safe and getting the help he needed. The whole conversation seemed like a nightmare. I knew years ago that something wasn't quite right with my father. Tears filled my eyes and I hoped desperately that he would be okay. To clear my head I hopped in my car and went for a drive. I parked my car at a local park by the campus and cried till I couldn't anymore. I was scared and I didn't know what to do. I decided that I didn't want people to judge me for what had happened. So, I never mentioned it to anyone and dealt with it all on my own. I didn't want the focus to be about my family or me. We had an SEC championship to win and I wanted to perform well. We needed to win to get a good NCAA tournament seed.

We entered the SEC tournament with a No.5 seed. We came out the first game with a much needed win against South Carolina. The next game would be more of a challenge. After playing pretty close the whole entire game we got an overtime win over LSU, 100-99. We were excited because they had beaten us in Baton Rouge earlier that season. We played with great passion and poise that game. We looked like the seasoned team of old. In the semifinal game we faced Auburn. Determined and ready, we stormed the court and battled back and forth the whole game. We gave everything, but came up short and lost 61-59. On the way home Coach didn't say a single word. We rode back to campus with heavy hearts and tears in our eyes.

After I got back to campus I received a phone call that Coach wanted to meet with me the next day. I knew this meeting was not going to be filled with pleasantries or congratulatory remarks. I knew she was displeased with how we had finished the tournament. She wanted to win just as much, if not more than we did. I sat down ready to hear whatever she had to say. She got on me about not leading the team and said it was my fault that we had lost. She said that I was playing scared. She hit me hard when she said, "That's why you probably won't win SEC Player of the Year, because other than that, no one is more talented than you." My blood boiled as I sat in that chair, but I knew she was trying to motivate me. She said that if I wanted to compete in this NCAA tournament, I better get it together, get my teammates to play with me and not be so distracted. She said, "Mique, you have to focus." I left her office fired up. The competitor in me wanted to make her eat her words. Maybe she was right. Maybe I had let what was going on with my family get the best of me. I went home cried and prayed. I was determined not to let anything or anyone break me. I was angry, not just about basketball, but because of what happened to my dad.

Right before the tournament we practiced and really worked on our execution. We learned how to get more energy from one another. Coach Summitt said that we needed to learn to play for each other and she was right. She told us to forget about what happened during the regular season. It's a new season, she stressed, "Let's go out there and play together and leave everything we got out there on the court." We ended up getting a No.3 seed. On a mission, we came out of the gate strong. In the Sweet 16 we met up with the No.2 seed, Colorado. To fire us up before this game the coaches put in our highlight tapes along with the songs "We Are the Champions" and "Eye of the Tiger." It did the trick and we upset Colorado, 75-67. We moved to the Elite 8 to face a Connecticut team who had embarrassed us in the previous meeting that year. We watched film and went over every Connecticut play. During the game, as soon as we heard their play or saw the signal, we knew exactly what they were running. We were very prepared and sharpened our game plan. We executed to perfection and defeated the No.1 seeded UConn, 91-81.

I can still remember the tears on the faces of our opponents as the buzzer sounded with the score in our favor. Tennessee had lit Carver-Hawkeye Arena on fire and Iowa City had witnessed great basketball. We were now headed to Cincinnati for the Final Four. We had weathered a bad storm and had the opportunity to be back-to-back NCAA champs. When we arrived home to Knoxville, the support was immeasurable. Our fans had weathered this storm with us. After briefly sleeping in our own beds we headed to Cincinnati. I remembered all the people who had counted us out and said we were lucky to be ranked in the Top 10. I was focused and ready to go. Pat met up with me before we headed out and said she wanted me to room with Kellie Jolly. She knew how big this game was and wanted me to remain focused. I was already 100% there, but I respected her and agreed. Besides, it would be good to have two leaders of the team firing one another up. We were now headed to Cincinnati as seasoned vets so all the hoopla couldn't distract us at all. All we could see in front of us was that trophy. We told the freshmen to stay focused. All the bright lights can be distracting, and we wanted to make sure we were a tight fist when we went in for the one-two punch.

This was by far my toughest season as a Lady Vol physically, emotionally and mentally. We had really struggled as a group and I'd often had to carry the load and try my best to bring it every night. I wasn't afforded the luxury of taking breaks. I know many people praised me for carrying the team that year, but I really couldn't have done it without my teammates. It's so much easier when you have people that genuinely support what the coaches say and play for each other. I can remember things like senior Pashen Thompson always telling me to run my players off her side because she would set a great screen and get me open. Senior Abby Conklin would tell me to run pick and rolls off her side when teams were doubling me because she was such a great pick and pop shooter. Even our freshmen, Kyra Elzy and Niya Butts, helped by wanting to lock down the other teams' best guards so that I didn't get burned out. Most importantly was Kellie Jolly, who would meet with me to discuss our game plans and where she thought I might be open as well as the secondary options. On my baseline screen she would say, "Mique, when you are running to Abby's side, run as hard as you can. You are my first option, but the whole arena thinks you are getting the ball. The other team is going to jump you and help and Abby or Pashen will be wide open for the duck in." We shared dialogue like this the whole season as we tried to figure it out. We knew we had a great leader in Coach Summitt, but the players were the ones that had to step out on the floor and play.

Through our ups and downs, we grew to understand each other's strengths and weaknesses. We had seen times when people had broken down in tears, frustrated. Some teammates had suffered injuries and wanted to be there, but couldn't, yet we still had their voices. We had gotten through it all and so we walked with a confidence no one could crush. We weren't leaving there without a title in our hands.

I was named a Kodak American for the second straight year. Our coaching staff and players were so proud of me. I will never forget that as I was leaving the banquet for the award, I overheard a group of people talking and I was angered by a gentleman who said that it was luck that Tennessee had beaten UConn and that we would lose in the semifinal matchup against Notre Dame. I was furious but at the same time thanked him for adding fuel to the fire. I wanted to prove him wrong as well.

The day before our semifinal showdown we had a film session that lasted for two hours. The coaches had food and snacks for us there so we would be focused. We discussed their every movement and how to contain their superstars, Beth Morgan, a sharp shooting small forward, and Katrina (Tree) Gaither, a fellow New Yorker who was an athletic rebounding machine at the 4 spot.

After the film I went to hang out with my teammates in their rooms, and on my way back I ran into Mickie DeMoss. I asked her what she was doing. She said, "Watching film with your momma." We would refer to Pat as "Momma" most of the time. I took a peek in the room and saw Coach Summitt with her glasses on. She was focused and hard at work. As players, whenever we saw Coach Summitt with glasses on, we were scared. Many of the players would say, "Oh Boy! It's that time of the month. Coach is going to ride us to death!" I joked that it was her split personality, Patricia Sue. This was when I really started to pay attention to just how hard she worked.

As soon as she saw me peek my head in, she said, "Hey Mique, come in and grab some of these snacks if you like. Sit down for a second I want to show you something on this video." I ended up watching some plays of me not finishing strong at the basket and not being strong with the ball. She told me not to shy away from the contact and to rip through with the ball to get players off me. This way, it would cut down on my turnovers and get me to the free throw line more.

After viewing the videos I headed back to my room. John Alpert and Maryanne De Leo, who were working on the HBO documentary, wanted to capture Kellie and me on tape talking about the big game tomorrow. So I sat on my bed as we excitedly talked about the game. That morning when I had gotten on the bus, Coach Summitt asked me how I felt. I told her fine. Coach Mickie DeMoss said, "Pat, you know Holdsclaw when she smells that popcorn in the building, she's ready to play." That was typical Mickie. Very witty with a well-timed joke. She always kept everyone loose and ready to play.

Soon it was game time and we were headed over to the arena. Everyone sat in their seats with their music on, but would turn it off to watch our highlight tape. Those same old songs, "We Are the Champions" and "Eye of the Tiger" pumped us up once again. As we exited the bus we knew it was time for business.

When you are playing in big situations like the Final Four, you can feel the adrenaline as it pumps through your veins. The first few minutes of the game are like a track meet until each team calms down. We played poised and well. I couldn't believe that this was the same team that had played in the regular season. We communicated and covered each other's backs. We ended up beating Notre Dame, 80-66. I remember the coaches told us before the buzzer sounded not to celebrate until we won tomorrow. As young kids overcoming a huge obstacle, we wanted to jump up and down and scream with excitement, but we handled it with class and moved on. Our sights were bigger and we still had business to take care of. In that locker room after the game there was nothing but joy. Coach Summitt said, "Doesn't it feel good?"

I had so many butterflies in my stomach and the night before the next game I tossed and turned. I was so ready to step on the court to play. And soon here we were on our way to play in another National Championship Game in front of a packed arena on National TV. We were headed to play Old Dominion, who had beat Stanford by one point 83-82. The game was led by sensational point guard, Ticha Penicheiro and Clarisse Machanguana, who stood at an imposing 6'5, a strong shot-blocking inside force. This team really had size and I knew we would have our work cut out for us. We had to be aggressive, but knew we may not get all the way to the basket with Machanguana there. With Ticha, we had to pressure her and try to make her into a scorer. She had an amazing ability to find the open player. Her passing ability and skill to create for others wasn't something we had seen a lot of. Coach Summitt said, "Make Penicheiro into a scorer and get Machanguana into foul trouble."

The game went back and forth, but we were playing well and reading each other like a book. I remember a play where Kellie threw me this lob/ally-oop type pass near the rim. I went up, got it and scored it with ease. It was so seamless that it looked like a drawn up play. We were able to get some energy from that play. Our defense picked up in the second half and we were able to get some easy scores. We started trapping Tichia and forcing her to give the ball up while denying her hard so that she couldn't get it back. We had started to wear down their superstar and we were making plays on both ends of the floor.

And so when the final buzzer sounded, we were back-to-back NCAA Champions, winning 68-59. We rushed each other and jumped up and down with great excitement. We were doing our dance of joy. I was so happy I was numb. This championship was a testament that when you roll up your sleeves and work hard, great things can happen. Not only had we worked hard, we worked smart. My grandmother was there supporting me and after the game, during an interview on national television I said, "I want to give a shout out to all my homies in Astoria and QB." My friends back at home still talk about it today. I'm so glad that I shouted them out because those people in the Astoria Projects and in Queensbridge were so proud of me. They stood by me and they lived the journey with me. The courts and the projects helped raise me and this was just as much their championship as it was mine.

When we arrived back in Knoxville the support was incredible. The fans had endured the season in the stands and we knew our winning meant so much. They always stuck with us. I remember talking to John and Maryanne from HBO and they said they were so relieved. They mentioned how they didn't know how things would turn out, having watched us go through one of our worst seasons. John said that it couldn't have been written any better, hence the title of the documentary: "The Cinderella Season."

Coach Summitt decided that we would do a big autograph signing at Thompson Boling Arena where we had played. It was our way of giving back. We wanted to do something for our fans, "The Orange People," as they are called. We had thought we were going to sign for an hour or two; however, that session ended up being more around six hours. There were so many people there and we wanted to make sure no one left without having something signed.

After we finished, a fan had somehow gotten through the roped area in the back of the locker room. He asked me for my autograph, but the officer escorting me in stopped him and ushered me away. A few days later we read about what had happened in the newspaper. It was written that I had been mean to the fan, which was far from the truth. Coach Summitt came to my defense and said that it was the officer who told the fan no. The officer had specific orders to get the players out of there after the session. I appreciated her coming to my defense; I have always been grateful of the people that have supported me.

My focus the rest of the year was sharp and I finished the school year with a 3.5 GPA. I had grown up tremendously. I learned what it meant to take full responsibility. I had been the responsible one in my household when my parents were going through their addiction issues. I was the one who made sure my brother was fed and bathed so that we could get up and go to school each day. However, this was different. I was doing something for *me* and it was something I loved.

As I reflected on my journey that season I looked through one of my old journals I saw that I had written, "I became more confident in my abilities and therefore, others became more confident in me." My family had taught me how to respect others, and myself but I was learning on my own and in the real world what life was all about. I was learning how to apply what I had learned. Coach Mickie DeMoss told me, "Holdsclaw, I'm going to cook you whatever you want because you played your heart out this season and grew up so much. On top of that, you have also become a better student." More than anyone Mickie really understood my struggles and could appreciate how far I'd come. It was Mickie who had me come to her office so that she could help me study. Mickie was that coach that I could talk to about anything.

CHAPTER 9

Love, Life & More Basketball

I had begun to date a guy from Hiwassee Junior College in Madisonville, Tennessee. His name was Markus Hallgrimson. Jeffrey Upton, one of Tennessee's football managers, had introduced us. That summer I had my mind set on attending the first session of summer school and then going home to NYC. My roommate, Kim Smallwood and I, went to visit him that same summer. Markus went to school with Jeffrey's brother, so we all hung out together. The first night we met we had some great conversations. At the end of it he mustered up the courage and asked me for my telephone number. We kept in touch daily and he would come up each weekend during summer school. I really enjoyed his company. He was sweet and we had so much in common; he also played basketball. On the nights when Kim wasn't there he would spend the night. We would snuggle together as we laughed and swapped life stories. I felt like I could really be myself with him. I started to develop strong feelings for him, as we grew closer. We had talked about being intimate, but he knew my concerns about becoming pregnant and that I was a virgin. So to protect myself I went to the campus clinic and began taking birth control. Soon afterward, I had my first intimate night with him. We had been hanging out all day in my dorm room spending time as we had in the weeks before. But that night one thing led to another and before I could fully realize what was happening, we were having sex.

I valued Mickie's opinion and I wanted her to meet the guy I was dating. So one day after lunch we stopped at her house so that she could meet him. Mickie seemed to like him. The conversation flowed and he had her laughing. We hung out there for a while and had a great time. I was pleased that I had her stamp of approval, or so I thought. A few days later I ran into Angela O'Neal, who was now working at the University in the Athletic Department. She said to me, "Girl, did Mickie talk with you?" I said, "No why?" Angela said, "I will just let her talk with you." I had no idea what she was talking about, but I shrugged and said, "okay."

The following week I was in the basketball office and Mickie was being her normal self. Then she closed her office door and said to me, "Holdsclaw, what are you doing?" I wasn't really sure what she was asking me. She then broke it down and told me that she didn't think Marcus was the one for me. I sat there in my seat and wondered if she had an issue with him because he was white. She said, "I just can't see ya'll together. Do you really like him?" I told her that I wasn't sure about my feelings for him. She encouraged me to be smart and to not get myself into anything that I couldn't get out of. Up until that day I hadn't really seriously considered the direction of our relationship.

After our chat I went back to my dorm to talk to Kim. I was shocked and told her, "Dang, Mickie doesn't like him!" She said, "Well, I don't either." I started to question what I was doing. Did they see something I didn't? These were people I trusted and I knew they were only saying this to protect me. I continued to see him for a few more weeks before I broke it off. When we broke up he had asked me if it was because he was white; I told him no and that I was open to dating whomever. I told him that the relationship was moving too fast and I didn't want to make a commitment.

Markus was kind about it, and we have kept in touch over the years. He's had a long successful career playing basketball in Europe and other countries. He is divorced now with beautiful twin daughters. He makes it back to the states each summer to visit his girls.

After summer school I wanted to spend time with my family, but Coach Summitt thought it would be a good idea for me to play USA Basketball. I would be playing on the 1997 World Championship Qualifying Team. I didn't have any international experience, but agreed to take on a new adventure. I had never been outside of the US, so that was something I was looking forward to. Prior to going overseas I went home for a short time to see my family. I needed to make sure all was well since I hadn't seen them since winning the championship.

While I was home I visited my dad in the hospital. I didn't know what to expect and was nervous about seeing him there. As I approached the doors of the facility that day my knees shook. I was thankful my grandmother had decided to come with me. We walked into reception with my grandmother's hand in mine, signed in and asked the nurse where we could find my father. We walked down the hall to the elevator to go up to the third floor where he was being treated. I pressed the button and waited for the doors to open as my heart pounded out of my chest. What would be on the other side of those doors? We walked into the room and I found my father staring out of the window. He looked like he was in a trance, the life gone from his eyes. I walked over to him as tears started to fill my eyes. The nurse could see the horror on my face and came to talk to me. She assured me that as long as he took his medicine and didn't drink he would be fine. Then my dad looked over at me and told me to stop crying. He said that everything would be okay. I wanted him to be better so badly. My mom was doing so well and I hoped the same for him. My grandmother comforted me as only she could, letting me know that stressing out would not help the situation. She reminded me that no family is perfect and told me to put my faith in God. Without her words I would have been buried by my fears. Though my time at home was short, I was grateful for it.

When I went back to Knoxville I had the room to myself for the rest of the summer. Kim decided that she wanted to be closer to home and had transferred to Rice, and Tiffani was living off campus. Now that I was alone I needed to make new friends. It was either that or stare at the walls until school started again in the fall. So I ventured outside of my comfort zone and hung out with my non-basketball friends. It was good for me to get outside the comfortable bubble of basketball. That summer I became good friends with Melanie Beaty, Antonio Brewer, and a fellow New Yorker, Zakiah Modeste. We would spend hours together doing our best to make the most out of being in Knoxville.

During summer school, my new friends and I worked Coach Summitt's camp. It was a lot of work, but we were happy about the money we were making and as a college student, every penny counted. Our Tennessee camps were packed with players from all over the globe. It was a fun experience having the opportunity to teach the game to the kids who idolized the Tennessee program and us. I was having an amazing time getting paid to do what I loved until I was called into Coach Summitt's office. She called me in during my break at camp and said, "Mique, I know you and Tiffani are close, but we are having an issue with her and some of her choices off of the court." She asked, "Do you know what is going on?" I said, "No" My wonder quickly turned into panic. I had no idea what was going on. I thought about everything we had done together as my heart started to beat faster and faster. My thoughts quickly turned to my grandmother and what she would say if I had unintentionally gotten myself involved in something bad. I didn't know what to think. I was completely clueless as to what Coach was talking about. My thoughts raced as I walked out of her office. She was clearly upset about something serious and I wanted no part of her wrath. I knew I had done nothing wrong, but I was shaken by her words.

The next day I got a call from Tiffani saying that Coach Summitt was greatly disappointed in the decisions she was making and that her actions had jeopardized her scholarship and her place on the team. Coach was thinking about suspending her. Whatever she had done was significant enough for it to have gone this far. Tiffani downplayed the situation. I was in the middle and wanted no part of whatever was going on. I did my best to put it out of my mind and moved on with my summer. Whatever was going on would have to be worked out by them. To keep my mind off the situation I did my best to stay busy. One night Zakiah, Melaine and I went to a party where we ran into Larry, my friend who worked at the West Town Mall Foot Locker. We had kept in contact and he looked out for me. Whenever I saw him we always had a lot to talk about and enjoyed each other's company, but because of the five year age difference I never looked at him as more than a friend—until that night.

I wasn't sure what to do with my feelings. Should I try to pursue a relationship or should I leave things as they are? Not knowing what to do I asked my good friend Vince for advice. He didn't want to hear about me and another guy but advised me anyway. He thought I should go for it if I thought he was the guy for me. Shortly after that, Larry and I were inseparable. Larry was about 6'5 and had an athletic body. He had played football at Knoxville College not too far from UT. We connected all across the board enjoying most of the same things. I even learned to accept that he had a child. He had gotten his girlfriend pregnant his freshman year in college and could not walk away from the responsibility. They could not work it out and be together, but he wanted to be a staple in the child's life. He was great with his son and I appreciated that about him. Getting to know him and his family made me fall for him hard. I admired the person I had come to know.

That summer we took things slow, but I knew Larry was the one for me. If I wasn't in class or on the court I was thinking of him. We were together all summer long until I left for USA Basketball. I felt something for him that I had never felt before. This was the first time I had ever cared deeply for someone outside of my family and friends. I could let my guard down and cry on his shoulder if I needed to. He was so uplifting and encouraging. Larry was a welcomed distraction that summer, taking my mind off whatever was going on between Coach and Tiffani. I started to pull away from her and go my own way because I didn't want to be in the middle of anything.

Tiffani and I had spoken a few times, but our friendship had changed in a blink of an eye. I was hearing rumors that some of the players thought I had "told on her" and was responsible for what had happened. I didn't know the entirety of what was going on. I was in the dark too. Pat moves in silence and is well connected. She has her ways of getting to the bottom of things and this situation was no exception. In the eyes of my teammates I was a "snitch." I did my best to defend myself, but some of them believed what they wanted.

I was happy it was time for USA Basketball and to get out of Knoxville and our team drama. I had to head down to Colorado Springs, Colorado to start training camp. I knew the intensity of being with the USA team would take my mind off of my team. Coach Fortner had all of us run a timed mile our second day there. That altitude almost killed me. The air was so thin I could feel my lungs burn with every breath I took. Somehow I was able to make my mile time at the required time of 6 minutes and 30 seconds. Practice was tough. I was playing with seasoned professional women playing in the American Basketball League (ABL) as well as overseas. I was intimidated at first, but after a few practices I became just one of the girls. I was the only college player on the team and the youngest of the group. Teresa Edwards, Katie Smith, Edna Campbell, Sylvia Crawley and Sheri Sam were a few of my teammates. I felt so honored to be in the company of such great players. I often found myself watching them instead of playing. When I was younger, Sheri Sam was one of my favorite players. She was so smooth and did everything with ease and here I was playing with her. Everyone was strong, everyone had great ability and everyone was great at what they did.

After training for several days we headed to Canada, Slovakia, and Germany. To help me through this experience, our coach, Nell Fortner, paired me in a room with veteran guard Teresa Edwards. She was the oldest and most experienced player on the team. I was nervous to room with her because she expected so much from me on the court. She would push me harder than anyone. She told me that because I was the youngest I was going to have to work harder than anyone else. Her determination was intimidating and you could never tell what was going on behind her eyes. She was a fierce competitor who never let up, and I respected her work ethic. On the court Teresa taught me some veteran tricks, like tucking the ball when I go in for lay-ups so that I wouldn't get stripped. She also got on me about rebounding the ball, being nervous and looking for the point guard. Teresa said, "Mique, you can dribble if you get rebound and no one is there. Push it up the court." She helped me to get over my nervousness on the court.

One time, I recall being in the hotel room listening to music and doing a crossword puzzle while she was reading. She pulled out a book and signaled for me to come over to the desk where she sat. She said, "Mique, you need to read this, here is a great book." She handed me a book about the Delany Sisters, two black women who were sisters who lived 100 years. The book was a storied history of the African American experience during their lifetime. The women were daughters of a slave and then became civil rights pioneers. I was so fascinated by their story and once I got home, I started asking questions that I had never asked before about my heritage. I wanted to know where my ancestors were from. I wanted to know more about being a black woman in this world and our struggles and triumphs as a people. It was on that trip that I fell in love with African American History.

My eyes were wide open and I wanted to experience and learn all I could from the places and women I was surrounded by. While on tour in Slovakia, we went to get ice cream after a game one night and a little boy approached me in the shop. The little boy looked at me, saying "Chocolate, chocolate." I asked him, "Do you want some ice cream?" He just smiled and pointed at my skin. He kept saying that I looked like chocolate. I thought to myself, "I must be the only black person he has ever seen." I was new to this place and this place was new to me. While we were there we also visited a natural spring. I was told that the people believed the water was a cure that could heal the body. I did my best to keep my mind open.

The qualifying tournament took us to Brazil and I had the chance to experience Sao Paulo and Rio de Janeiro. They were both beautiful cities full of life and energy. You could feel the spirit of the country through the music and vivid colors. It was one of my favorite places. We played Cuba in the semifinals of the tournament on my twentieth birthday. For my gift teammates gave me Pampers, but on the court I didn't play like a baby. I scored 32 points and added 7 boards, in a tough 94-90 win that got us to the finals. We lost to their national team in front of a packed crowd. The trip didn't end how we would have liked, but I remember Coach Fortner telling me to keep my head high and that I should be proud of how I had played. I led the team in scoring and rebounding 19.0 ppg and 6.2 rpg. I was excited and disappointed all in the same moment. The work I had put in paid off, but we came home without winning and there was nothing I hated more. Still, I was eager to get home and check out the other books I had heard about over my trip.

When I arrived back in New York, my grandmother and I had a lot of catching up to do I wanted to tell her all about my experience traveling the world. I told her about the book I had read and she was very impressed. Each summer when I was a child she used to make me pick out a book to read and do a report on. I would complain about it, so it was refreshing for her to see me reading books at my leisure now.

All around, I had a fun eventful summer. It went by quickly and with a little more than a week before classes started, I decided to go home to West Virginia with my friend Melanie Beaty. She happened to be dating a mutual friend, but he would often cheat on her. She would call me to help her go and spy on him. It was the funniest mess at the time. One time, she suspected that he had some girl over. She knew that he would keep one of his windows open. She called me so that I could help her go and climb a tree and get into his apartment. Let's just say that she got in and found out he had company. Till this very day I tell her that she almost got me put in jail for trespassing.

I was excited to be finally moving off campus and decided to move in with Zakiah, who had become my close friend over the summer. She was a triple jumper for the women's track team so she understood the demand of sports. After the situation with Tiffani I didn't want to live with another teammate and Zakiah felt the same way. We both appreciated each other's time commitment and all that came with being a student athlete. We moved about two miles from campus into a townhouse. It felt great to live with someone who really understood where I came from. We got along great even though Zakiah and I were complete opposites. She was full of energy and outgoing while I was more laid back and shy. She brought me out of my shell and I helped her to be more focused. She was a great student, but wore so many different hats. I used to say that she was a "student athlete by day, spoken-word artist and entertainer by night." I had always played it safe, so being roommates with Zakiah was a welcomed adventure.

Zakiah was from the suburbs of Mount Vernon, New York, and didn't live far from Phylicia Rashad who had played Claire Huxtable on *The Cosby Show*. She came from a middle class neighborhood; both her parents were educators who immersed her in an environment rich with artifacts, statues, paintings and educational materials that were reflective of their cultural heritage. Her dad's hobby was refereeing basketball in NYC. He was big on using sports as a vehicle to develop, teach and educate inner city youth. He was also aware of my basketball career. Zakiah had told me that when she was indecisive about where to attend college her dad said, "Look, this girl is going to Tennessee. You should check it out" and showed her an entry that I had written for the *NY Daily News*. Intrigued by what I had written she decided to come to Tennessee. She was majoring in consumer science with a minor in theater. If you ask me, Theater should have been her major. She was the type of person that could command the attention of anyone. She has the unique ability to entertain a crowd. She could be all over the place and still maintain a 3.0 GPA or better with ease.

To say the least, I was ready for the upcoming year. I was excited about my new roommate and about our New York connection and the relationship that had developed between Larry and me. We had kept in contact the whole summer, talking every day even when I was abroad and our connection was stronger than ever. Once I was back at school we had spent almost every single day together and things were moving fast. He had already graduated, but decided to stay in Knoxville to be with his son. He started working for the city of Knoxville and although he knew he would have more opportunities in Chicago where he was from, he didn't want to leave. I respected that he stayed. My thoughts at a young age were that I didn't want to date a man who had kids, but my opinions changed once Larry entered my life. He was special and I wanted to see where our relationship was headed.

CHAPTER 10

The Three Meeks

It was time to welcome our incoming freshman class and everyone was excited. I knew these four players were special. Each player gave us something that we didn't have. Kristin "Ace" Clement was an athletic lefty point guard who was able to score and had great size with the ability to make amazing no-look passes. Semeka Randall was a strong, aggressive, in-your-face defender who was a force in the open floor. Teresa Geter, also known as Big Smooth, made it look easy in the paint, like it took no effort at all. Last, but not least was Tamika Catchings, an athletic 3/4 player. She was a hard-nose defender with a nice outside shot that could run the floor with great ease. Individually their abilities were great, but collectively we had the chance to do something special. I did my best to get them acclimated to college life. I wanted to make sure they were as comfortable as possible when they arrived. I was hoping to save them the angst I went through as a freshman. I knew how important they were going to be to this team so I did what I could to ease the transition.

For the first time since I had been at UT, I now had a life outside of basketball. I was fully settled in Knoxville and it was starting to feel like home. The days of hanging around campus and being bored in the dorms were over since I now lived off campus. I went to class, to the gym and then home. If I wasn't hanging out with my boyfriend Larry, I was with my new friends. I wanted to find balance between doing what I loved and being a student and friend. Basketball had fully consumed me my first two years at UT and I was starting to feel like I was missing out on the full college experience. I wanted to make sure I was growing outside of my sport too. I found myself spending less and less time with my team outside of practice. Plus, the team had no idea what I dealt with in the weeks prior to coming to school. Coach Summitt had decided to dismiss Tiffani Johnson from the team for good.

When Tiffani called me and told me that Pat had officially dismissed her from the team my heart sank. Despite all that had happened between us, I still wanted her on the team and as my friend. I asked her what she had done to be in this situation. She said that she didn't do anything wrong and that Pat had made her decision based on rumors she'd heard about the people she had been hanging out with. I told her that if what she said was true, I would go and talk to Coach on her behalf. So I went to Pat I pleaded to her about how much we needed Tiffani and how Tiffani wanted to be here at Tennessee. Pat combated my pleas by saying that she had worked too hard to build this program and that she wasn't going to let anyone's poor choices compromise that. She said that the young freshman required good role models and that her decision was final. She went on to say that we would be okay as a team and that I would be impressed by how much the freshmen would help us. After talking with Coach, I walked out of her office knowing I had just lost a good friend. Once everything was decided I did my best to keep in touch with Tiffani, but it was not the same. It was a tense situation and it hurt me that some of the players felt I had something to do with her not being there. There was an obvious separation between my team and me, but it wasn't for the reasons they thought.

I grew tired of always having to defend myself and hearing the whispers of what people thought I had done. So one day I confronted the person who supposedly had been calling me a snitch. It was denied that I was ever called that, so I let it go and moved on. I knew that something like this would just further divide us and hurt our chances of being successful on the court. They were my sisters and we were all close in our way. Coach Summitt would often say, "There are some people on your team that you would take to dinner, but not to war." I wanted to be able to take every one of my teammates to war, but I knew underneath the surface there was a clear divide. So I separated myself from the team and the freshmen soon felt the result of the unresolved friction between us. They didn't appreciate the sudden cold shoulder and it showed during our first team meeting.

The freshmen expressed how they had come here to play with me, but I wasn't helping them or living up to what I had promised them during their visits. I didn't say much at all that meeting. I just listened and I took responsibility for my actions. I had helped convince these girls to come and play with me, so if I had to give them more I was okay with that. I apologized and tried to make them understand that my newfound independence had nothing to do with a lack of care for them. I wanted them to know I was there for them and if they ever needed me I was just a phone call away. When they told me how they had felt that day in the meeting, I knew I had to change how I approached the situation. I couldn't let some people's opinions of me affect who I was as a person or who I was to them.

As I was leaving the meeting that day Kellie pulled on my arm and said, "Mique, it's okay. Don't you worry about it." I thanked her for trying to understand where I was coming from. Kellie Jolly knew how settled I had become. She also knew that I didn't like the tension any more than my teammates did. Kellie was the type of person that you would meet and instantly know that she would be successful. She had great work ethic and charisma. My years at Tennessee would not have been the same had she not been there.

Once we hit the court for individual workouts and I saw the intensity the four freshmen brought to the table, I knew we were going to be a special team. They were eager to learn and ready to go. The ten losses from last season were still fresh in my mind and I knew with the help of the freshmen we would get the payback we deserved. Each day we worked harder than the last. We held each other accountable and pushed past our limits. The want for greatness was contagious.

The critics had a lot to say about our team and I knew most of them wondered if we had the staying power to remain on top. From the first day of practice it was clear that we had the potential to be great and I truly felt we were the best. We had so much athleticism and skill, and on top of that we were coached by the best, Pat Summitt. Some of the plays we made that year rivaled the men's team.

While playing at Oregon during the preseason I remember us making one such play. I rebounded the ball and out of the corner of my eye I saw Semeka running the opposite lane pointing up. I pushed the ball to half court as she broke away from her defender and lobbed the ball up. She caught the pass while in the air and laid it in. Our team was poetry in motion. Spin moves and behind the back passes were a regular part of our games. There were even times when it looked like Tamika and I were playing volleyball out there as we tapped the ball back and forth to each other while grabbing rebounds. We were hard-nosed and aggressive. I often found myself in awe of some of the plays we would make. We played so well together that we soon developed the moniker "The Three Meeks." There wasn't a play that season that didn't involve one of us and when we were on the floor together, nothing could stop us. We were a balanced team with a smooth inside/outside attack. We used our great athleticism to create a smothering defense. We wreaked havoc, but most importantly we worked hard and took nothing for granted.

Coach pointed out that I had to be aggressive and lead the way in order for us to be as successful as we wanted. I accepted the challenge and put the team before myself. I believed that if we all worked together, it would be possible for all of us to shine. As the season progressed we blew out teams left and right. During the last season, I'd said I didn't want to go through anything like that again. It was long and I had most of the weight on my shoulders. However, this year was different; the load was shared equally between my teammates and me. Each of us believed there wasn't an opponent that could match us. We had a confidence that could not be shaken, but mainly because we pushed one another to be better every day. We were called "America's Team" and had a huge following no matter where we went.

Right before we began tournament play, our HBO documentary was released and we had a prescreening at the Tennessee Theater. We all had to get dressed up in black-tie attire. The prescreening of *A Cinderella Season: The Lady Vols Fight Back* was attended by 1,500 invited guests and was a great event. The cheerleaders cheered us on as we entered and fans screamed in support. Each of us got to reflect on the trials and tribulations we endured that year. We had gone through so much as a team to get to this point and we were all grateful to be in a better standing this season. The screening motivated us to stay on top.

Our season was storybook from beginning to end capped off by a perfect record of 39-0. Even though we put together a great season and I played well, I found comfort in knowing that if I didn't play my best, I still had players like Tamika and Semeka who could step in and help get the job done. We had no egos, just a group that wanted to make something special happen and we did. We ended up winning our sixth title for the University of Tennessee and my third consecutive at the Final Four in Kansas City, Missouri, at Kemper Arena. We defeated Louisiana Tech 93-75 in the championship game. The media attention we received as a team was unheard of for a women's college basketball team. The media questioned me throughout the season and frequently asked if I would come back for a fourth season. I often laughed to myself, thinking that these folks did not know my grandmother and that there was no way I was leaving Knoxville without a degree. With success of the ABL and the start of the WNBA, many said I could have created a bidding war. I guess when I didn't comment about the speculation people took that as me being interested. Little did they know that what they were saying was the furthest thing from my thoughts. I had no intentions of leaving early and assured Coach Summitt that it wasn't even a consideration.

Tamika, Semeka, and I became the first trio from one college to be named Kodak All-Americans. We were truly humbled by the honor and excited that they appreciated all the hard work we had put into the season. Shortly after winning the title, Kellie and I went on the *Rosie O'Donnell Show* in NYC with Coach Summitt. Coach had authored a book called *Raise the Roof,* which was an inspiring story of our undefeated season. Lots of great things were happening for our program at Tennessee and for me personally. *TV Guide* put me on the cover of their special Brooklyn/ Queens edition and *Sports Illustrated* had given me the cover of a collector's edition after winning my third consecutive championship.

It was hard to stop and catch my breath I was flying so high.

I guess I was
born to ball

My mother,
grandmother
and brother

Me and my
brother Davon

I was so happy
with my Menudo
button

School picture
Age 6

Davon and I chilling

My grandma
June

After church with
grandmother,
brother, and
Uncle Thurman

Me age 12

Some of my
youth trophies

My father Willie

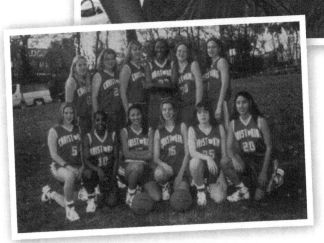

Christ the
King Team

High School
graduation 1995

My freshman
year in dorm
at UT.

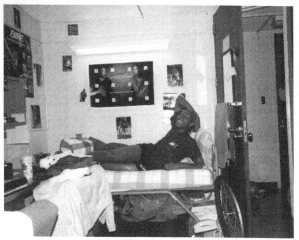

With my grandmother
after a college game

My grandmother
and H.S. Coach

At Final Four
in Charlotte
1996 with
grandmother
and brother

College
graduation with
Kellie and Jerry

Visiting friends
in Oklahoma

At lake in
Vegas with
my mother

Tennessee
Greats
(Chamique,
Peyton,
Peerless)

Soccer great
Mia Hamm

MCI Center
with Actor
Chris Rock

2006 Breast
Cancer walk in
San Francisco

Lady Vol
Hall of Fame
Induction with
Coach Summitt

Chamique with
Active Minds Staff

At physical
therapy with
Hank Aaron

Picked up a hat
in Russia

Hanging with my girls at a UT game

Community Service with friends

CHAPTER 11

As Real as It Gets

Through all the success I had during that season, Larry was right by my side. I now loved him dearly. He had become a huge part of my support system. Zakiah didn't really care for him much at first, but she knew how much he meant to me so she gave him a chance. She was protective of me and didn't want anyone being with me for the wrong reasons. I loved that he was a God-fearing man and he always made sure I was okay and made me feel special. He was a really good person and I felt lucky to have him. I was happy to have someone to share my successes and failures with.

Growth was the key and I was doing a great job at balancing my schoolwork, basketball, my social life, and all the pressures. I was being pulled in different directions, yet some how I was able handle it all. If it was up to me, I would have just gone to school and played ball, but there was so much more to it. I was becoming a household name and a role model. People didn't want to just see me; they wanted to listen to my words. As coach Summitt once said to me, "Everyone wants a piece of Chamique." She explained the importance of the responsibility I now had and how I had to embrace it. I didn't care about doing interviews or having my face on magazines; I just wanted the rings. It didn't really hit me until one day I was walking into West Town Mall and a woman and her husband signaled for my attention. Once I noticed, I walked over to them. They wanted to tell me how they were big supporters and how much they appreciated me. The lady was so happy and seemed to be on the verge of tears. She was pushing a stroller and said, "You have to meet my little girl." The baby was no more than six months old with blonde hair and big blue eyes. She looked at me and said, "We named our daughter after you meet Chamique." I was honored that someone thought enough of me to name their child after me. It touched my heart and from then on I had a true understanding of what I meant to others. My talent made people happy, excited and inspired. It's now been about twelve years since I graduated from college, and I have received several messages on my Facebook page from children whose parents had named them after me. It is truly humbling to be viewed with such great admiration.

The summer after my junior year at Tennessee I had World Championships with USA basketball. I was really excited because this time I would be playing with some of the biggest names in women's basketball: Lisa Leslie, Sheryl Swoopes, and Dawn Staley. After talking with my coaches they felt that it would be a great opportunity. So I decided to head home to NYC to see my family for a week before I met up with the team for training.

Before I left Knoxville for the summer I met with my academic advisor, Kerry Howland. We wanted to make sure I had everything in order so that I could graduate the following May. I was on track and the classes that I needed within my major would all be offered in the fall of my senior year. After our meeting Kerry and I sat there and laughed for a while. The beginning of college had been rough and both of us appreciated how far I had come. I had overcome the many hurdles throughout my academic career and was one the verge of graduation. I was swollen with pride at what I was about to accomplish. I was going to be able to fulfill the promise I had made to my grandmother and I couldn't have been happier.

Everything was in place for me to graduate, so I decided not to attend summer school. After the World Championships were finished, I felt I needed New York and the bright lights to restore me. I wanted to reconnect with the people I had lost in the shuffle over the years. I had unintentionally grown apart from so many people. I didn't want people to think that I had changed because of the success I had. I could not wait to return to the streets that had raised me.

Just before I was to head home I called my grandmother and told her of my plans for the summer. She excitedly answered the phone and told me she could not wait for me to get home. She loved when I was there; her house felt big and empty when I wasn't. I told her I was going to drive to New York with my boyfriend because I wanted her to meet him. The conversation shifted and I could hear the concern.

"Boyfriend? Who is this guy Chamique?"

I said, "Grandma, it's my boyfriend and he's coming home with me." She finally said it was okay. Early the next morning I received a phone call that woke me from my sleep. It was my grandma and she sounded really upset. She said, "Chamique, I just had a dream you were pregnant. Are you pregnant?" I told her no and to relax. I reassured her that I was fine and that it was just a bad dream. I said, "Look, I'm responsible and I'm fully aware that I am in no position to take care of a child." I got off the phone and wondered where this was all coming from.

My grandmother was still very weird about what she had dreamed when we arrived in New York and she refused to allow Larry to stay at her house. She simply said, "I don't want him here." All he could say was, "Chamique, I don't want to get between you and your grandmother." So out of respect, we went and stayed in Staten Island with my mom. It was actually nice to stay with my mom. I no longer looked upon her with shame, but with appreciation for staying strong in her fight to stay sober.

My dad had just started a rehab program and because of the visitation rules we didn't get to spend much time with him, but the time we did get was special. He was so happy to see me and kept saying, "My baby is growing up." My dad and Larry connected right away and had great conversations about me growing up. My dad was happy I was with someone who respected and cared for me. He wanted nothing else but to see me smile.

The trip to New York turned out to be great. Even my grandmother came around and decided to meet Larry. She was still cold at first but opened up a little bit and started to see what I saw in him.

I was glad she came around: it would have been impossible to stay in a relationship with someone my grandmother didn't approve of. She said, "We have spent so much time together, Chamique, and I have watched you grow into a beautiful young woman. I just don't want anyone to hinder you, but I trust you and I know for the most part, you make good decisions. Just don't change. Keep being the Chamique that I know humble and sweet." I hugged my grandmother and told her how much I loved her. Just before we left, she even hugged Larry and told him to take care of me.

On the way back to Knoxville Larry said, "You know what? Coming home with you and meeting your family has really helped me understand you as a person." I got defensive and said, "What do you mean by that?" He told me to calm down and said, "Miss June loves you so much and so does your mom. You are definitely a mixture of both." I said with a laugh, "No, I'm my father's child."

Larry said, "Chamique, you look like your father, but you have your grandmother's demeanor and her heart. She is very observant, very laid back and chill. And then there's that other side that is your mom all day." I sat there confused. He said, "Once you are comfortable with your surroundings and people, your mom comes out of you. You are very protective of the people you love, almost territorial." I told Larry to shut up, but I knew he was right. I did love hard and cared deeply for those who I let close to me. I have always prided myself on being a great friend and made sure I was there for those that needed me.

After our trip to New York, I headed to Colorado to the USA training facility to start preparing. It was intimidating at first, just as it had been the last time. All I could think about was being on the same team with Sheryl Swoopes. She had her own shoe and a Nike poster. I had it in my room and as far as the women's game was concerned, players like her, Lisa Leslie, and Dawn Staley, were all icons. Even though we were sponsored by Converse my first two years at Tennessee, I wore Nike, in particular, Sheryl's shoe, because they were so comfortable. I remember some people tried to make a big deal of it, but Coach Summitt said that her players had to wear what was comfortable on their feet. I had orthotics, but when you wear a women's size 14 and your feet are as narrow as mine (AAA), it's all about comfort. I remember Nike had sent me some white and red Swoopes to wear for USA basketball and I found myself caught in a dilemma. I didn't want to seem lame wanting to wear her shoe. I remember questioning myself, "Chamique, should I be wearing my teammate's signature shoe?" But in the end I didn't care because they felt good on my feet.

Unfortunately, Sheryl was injured and would not play with us that year, so the coaches were expecting more from me. When we started practice the intensity stepped up several notches. Luckily, I had a relationship with Teresa Edwards who I had played with the year before and I felt comfortable asking her for advice. She told me to work hard and keep rebounding. She said to bring energy when I stepped onto the court. I didn't have to worry about scoring because I had some great players around me. Each practice got better, but I knew that I had to get stronger. Physically, I was taking a beating, and it was starting to show. I felt like everyone was trying to coach me, but I guess that's what happens when you are the youngest member of the team. I took it all in because I didn't want to be disrespectful, but I really just wanted to find my own way. I knew I wouldn't be perfect, but I wanted to learn to fall and pick myself up.

After training for a week we got a few days off to go home and get our bags packed for the long journey aboard. Those days flew by and before I knew it I was flying to meet up with the USA team. Just before we left we practiced to tighten up some things and to make sure we were ready. We stopped in several countries to scrimmage teams before we headed to Germany. We had scrimmages in other cities to help us prepare for the big games that were ahead of us, and then we headed to the main event in Berlin. When we arrived we met up with friends and family who had flown in to support us. USA basketball paid for one of our guests, and because my grandmother didn't want to fly that long, I invited Larry. I often felt like a fish out of water, so it was great to have someone there who knew me.

I started the trip off strong, but as the games went on I grew fatigued and my game started to suffer. The trip was beginning to take a toll on my body. Mickie DeMoss, my assistant coach from Tennessee, met up with us and was there to support me. Before one particular game she said to me, "Mique, I know you are tired, but just get out there and have fun. You are playing like a robot. I'm tired of all these people talking crap and saying your shot doesn't look good and that you are playing tired." As always, I took that as a challenge, went out there and played a great game. She was so proud of me and said, "Mique, that's how you shut people up."

The stretch of two or three games where I didn't play like I could have caused Coach Fortner to move me out of the starting lineup. I would be coming off the bench once we got to the main stage. She told me to remain confident despite coming off the bench and that the team needed me. I knew I could play at that level and wanted to show what I could do. Even though I was a small forward, I was one of the best rebounders in the game. I have always had a knack for knowing when the ball was going to come off the rim. On the offensive end, I had to come off picks strong and get to the middle of the floor so that the defense would have to react to me. I knew my worth and wanted to quiet the naysayers who thought I didn't belong or that I wasn't ready.

As a team we went out there and played well. I did a great job coming off the bench and brought energy and effort into the game with me each time I stepped on the floor. The other teams could not match up with us and we walked away the gold medalist of the 1998 FIBA World Championships. We went 9-0 and I was third on the team in scoring and rebounding (10.9 ppg and 5.4 rpg).

I couldn't stop thinking about one of the games when I went 0-10 from the floor missing every shot I took. I was my own worst enemy that game. I beat myself up every time I made a mistake and it showed. I uncharacteristically missed lay-ups and easy shots. I was so disappointed that I had let fatigue take over me. During this trip I discovered a phase of my game that needed work and I was sure that I would be ready next time around. After talking with Larry, I felt better about things and realized I was happy to have been given such a great opportunity. Instead of trying so hard not to make mistakes, I should have been free and having fun. I put a lot of pressure on myself for no reason. Coach Fortner hugged my neck after the game and told me she knew it was tough. She was proud that I had pulled through. She told me to continue to work hard and to try to take something positive from each experience.

We headed back home to the states and I could not wait to get home to New York. I felt like I needed to refocus and work on getting stronger. I felt weak playing with the veterans of USA basketball and never wanted to feel that way again. All I could think about was having this time off in New York to prepare myself for my senior season. I was more focused and determined than ever. My plan was to work out at the Boys and Girls Club and my old high school throughout the week while also running on the track twice a week doing the programs our strength coach had given us. I really wanted to go out with a bang and I knew I was going to have to work for it.

One of my good family friends who was brought up playing with my Uncle Thurman worked at Chelsea Piers. Chelsea Piers was an amazing sports and training complex located in Manhattan. There were a lot of celebrities and professional athletes who worked out there. Our friend had mentioned to my grandmother that he could add me as family and I could go to the gym to work out. So I took advantage of the offer and worked out up there three times a week.

One day I was in the gym going about my work when in walked Jay-Z and Damon Dash. I was so excited I could have burst out of my skin. I am a huge fan, but I kept my cool and acted like it wasn't a big deal. They were often up there doing boxing workouts. I wanted to say hello, but I didn't want to interrupt their workout. I had just finished playing pickup and was shooting by myself. Jay-Z sat on the bleachers and started talking to me. He bet that I couldn't make 20 free throws in a row. I thought to myself, *Piece of cake, I can make 20 free throws in my sleep.* I step up to the line, confidently shot my free throw and clank went the ball off the back of the rim. I collected the ball, stepped back on the line and shot. Clank! I missed again. I quickly became frustrated. I was shocked that I kept missing shots that I could make with my eyes closed. All the while he sat back on the bleachers with a smug I-told-you-so look. I guess the pressure of performing for one of my favorite rappers got to me.

Still, I loved going up there to work out and play pickup with the guys. Some of the best moments that summer were spent in that gym. It was so much fun and I never knew who I might see while I was there. Gabrielle Reece, a pro volleyball player, model, actress and fitness guru, used that gym to stay in shape too. She was so kind and offered smart advice. She and her husband Laird, a professional surfer, were always pleasant and didn't act like the superstars that they really were. They were so down to earth.

New York City is the basketball mecca. The courts are always filled during the summer with games or neighborhood pick up. There is so much talent that passes through our courts. Zakiah, who happened to be home for the summer as well, would go watch the guys play at Hunter College and at the Rucker with me. It seemed like every time I sat down to watch a game that summer an agent would approach me. I was the first female basketball player to garner that much attention. I just remember my grandmother warning me, "Chamique, don't take anything from anyone." I was offered cars and apartments downtown for the summer, shoes and jewelry. You name it; I was offered it. All I had to do was make a commitment to sign with them.

I was at Rucker Park hanging out one day and a street agent came over to me and said, "How does it feel to be a millionaire?" I said, "I wish I knew. He said, "Holdsclaw, stick with me and you will be!" I must admit it was tempting, especially when I saw the nice cars and all the flash. I was shocked that these guys wanted to talk with me. I just saw myself as a girl who loved to play, not as a future millionaire. It all sounded good, but my grandmother's words stuck in my head and never left. I knew I couldn't take anything from anyone.

One day as I was watching Ron Artest play in the summer league, I ran into the famous Riverside Church founder, Ernie Lorch. He told me that he didn't watch women's basketball a lot, but had the chance to see me play. He thought I was a special player and that I had a bright future ahead of me. This was a huge compliment coming from him. Anyone that has ever played in New York knows that the church has had many great players go through their program. I really appreciated his words because I knew he knew basketball and had been around talented players his whole career.

During that summer my grandmother was also the recipient of promises of money, cars and homes by agents who wanted to represent me. She received phone call after phone call from people trying to get close to her in hopes that I would sign with them. Since then I've had people run into me and say, "Mique, I used to talk to your grandmother all of the time and try to get her to have you sign with me." My grandmother would politely listen, but she never even mentioned these people to me. Anyone who knew my grandmother knew that she wouldn't do anything to jeopardize my eligibility at Tennessee and did things strictly by the book.

When I was younger, friends from the block who hustled would look out for me and get me the newest Jordan's, but my grandmother would make me give them back. Her thing was you never knew what people wanted in return. It used to annoy them, these people I had known for a long time. I didn't understand why I couldn't accept a gift from an old friend, but as I have gotten older and wiser I have a clearer understanding of where she was coming from. As usual, she was just protecting me from myself and everyone else.

The summer went by quickly, but I felt like I had accomplished a lot. I was running, lifting and working on my game while enjoying some time at home. In my eyes it was the prefect summer that had given me just what I needed to recharge my battery. I was ready to hit the ground running my senior year. I had huge hopes and dreams for my last season in a Lady Vol uniform.

When I arrived at my apartment in Knoxville, Larry was there to greet me and help me unpack. Though we hadn't been apart for long, I had really missed him. We had spent nearly everyday together, and when I wasn't with him it felt like something was missing. As we were unpacking my things in my apartment Larry suddenly dropped down on his knee. I was initially confused by what was going on, thinking he had fallen over a box in my room. It was until I heard the words leave his mouth that I fully understood what was going on. He asked me to marry him and lifted a box from his pocket. I was so shocked when he opened the box and gave me the ring. I started to cry and emphatically said yes. I said yes over and over and kept telling him how much I loved him.

He said, "Are you sure?" I told him yes and told him not to ask me that again. I was 100% sure. After a long hug and a passionate kiss I called my family to tell them the news. They were supportive and happy for me. I was glad that they had gotten the chance to know him a little over the summer. It was important for me for him to know my family and for my family to know him. My grandmother was happy for me, but urged me not to get married until I graduated college. She wanted me to settle into life once I figured out what my career path would be. I agreed.

I then told Angela O'Neal and Mickie. They both knew how much I cared about Larry and they liked him, but deep down I knew they wondered what his intentions were. I was young and at times a little naïve, so they had to make sure I understood what had just happened. After I told them I went and talked to Coach Summitt. She told me to take my time and not to be in a rush. If it was meant to be, it would happen. Larry and I didn't plan on getting married until after I was done with school. The last thing he ever wanted was to distract me my commitments. And primarily, that was basketball.

CHAPTER 12

Final Year

Each piece of the puzzle seemed to come together as I entered my final year at UT. I had come full circle and matured greatly since coming to Knoxville. I never imagined that such a place would become a second home. Zakiah and I had moved into an apartment building near campus. It was a far cry from where we lived the year before. We moved from the party scene into suburbia. It was a quiet complex that mostly housed graduate students.

My grandmother was friends with our football star, Jamal Lewis' dad. They had actually been longtime friends in New York, which Jamal and I were not aware of. I guess during one of their conversations, he had mentioned to my grandmother that I should get an insurance policy through Lloyd's of London. My grandmother gathered up all the information, and my Uncle George looked into it. After requesting the information and talking me through everything, they agreed that it was in my best interest to get the policy in case I had a career-ending injury. In the case I couldn't play again, according to the policy, I would receive the sum of $1 million. I'm not going to lie and say that having that policy didn't make me feel better. I would hear stories about athletes on the brink of stardom that got injuries, and then down the tube went their dreams of helping their family financially and improving their lives. So that took some of the pressure off me and made me even more determined.

After we settled into our new apartment, Zakiah and I decided to get, of all things, a dog. We impulsively went down to the pet shop and bought an adorable little yellow lab. He had big brown eyes and floppy ears and we fell in love with him. We decided to name him Rolex. Neither of us had any experience raising dogs, but we were up for the challenge. Little did we know that taking care of a puppy is a lot of work, way more than either of us bargained for. He would chew anything he could get his paws on, especially my shoes. We also didn't realize that most dogs don't come potty trained, and our apartment soon became his personal toilet. Anytime he had to go to the bathroom he propped up his leg and went. Our new apartment started to smell like a kennel. He would wake us up super early wanting to play or go to the bathroom. Then we found out that while we were gone during the day, he would bark the whole time and the neighbors started to complain about it. We weren't really sure what to do. We wanted to keep him and found ourselves between a rock and a hard place. The turning point came when we arrived home to find an eviction notice on our door. We had received too many complaints about the dog and had to move.

It broke my heart to have to get rid of him, but it was necessary. I hadn't fully thought out all of the responsibilities that came with taking care of him. So I talked to some friends and asked if they knew anyone who could take him. One of my good friends knew a doctor in town who wanted to get a dog for his children. It wasn't easy to let him go, but we decided it was best for him to grow up in a home with a yard where he could run free. Now that we had found Rolex a new home, we had to find one for ourselves. School had already started and it was going to be difficult to find a good apartment that was still available. So in between school and practice we looked for a place to call home. We ended up finding an apartment out in West Knoxville. It was farther from campus than either one of us would have liked but offered us more space and was near the mall.

Thankfully, things on the court were going much smoother than they were at home. Workouts were going well and each of us looked forward to starting games. We welcomed our freshman center, Michelle Snow, who towered above us at 6'5. She had a slender build but aggressively played larger than her size. On her recruiting visit to UT, the team and I were waiting to eat with her in Gibbs Hall when she walked in. She had headphones around her neck and her pants sagging below her waist. She coolly gave us a nod and sat down at another table. I wasn't sure what to think, but I knew she had to be good if our coaching staff wanted her.

Coach Summitt noticed her jeans also and in a nice way took off her belt and told Michelle to put it on. She also asked her to take off the headphones. Michelle then joined us at the table. Out of all the recruits I had met with throughout my career, she probably had the least to say on her visit. It was hard to tell if she liked us or not. Everyone was happy when she committed to play with us. We excited to have another strong force in the paint. There was something about her that reminded me of myself. She too was shy, but under all of that was a confidence that emerged when she took the court.

After workouts one day she told me how she wanted to go home and that she really missed her family. She mentioned how she didn't have the money to take a flight home or have a car to drive. I knew how she felt; it hadn't been easy for me either. So on our free weekend before the season was to start, I volunteered to drive her from Knoxville, TN to Pensacola, FL. During our trip I learned a lot about Michelle. She told me that her mom had Lupus and that the illness was getting progressively worse. She was the oldest child, and took on much of the responsibility. To help her mother so she would take care of the household duties such as laundry and cooking. Once we arrived at the family's home, they thanked me over and over again. They had missed her just as much as she had missed them. I told them it was my pleasure. I could sympathize with her because of how homesick I had been during my first year.

Her family was a tight knit group and the love between them was palpable. It wasn't until I met her family that I fully understood who Michelle was. She had a big heart and gave so much of herself to her family. I admired her selflessness and appreciated that she allowed me into her world. From that day forward I wanted to be her family away from home.

Our team was feeling more like a family too. We were having fun and we were spending a lot of time together outside of basketball. Our sisterhood showed in everything that we did. I'm sure that if Coach Summitt were asked which teams had been easiest to coach, she would say the 1997-1998 and the 1998-1999 teams. We played with great intensity and passion. We played for each other every day. To keep us from getting complacent, though, Coach would still ride us. Whenever there was a misstep she was there to let us know about it. There were still days when I would find myself in the locker room upset because of something Coach Summitt said to me. In general, we were confident, but not cocky. Players curbed a piece of themselves for the betterment of the team and it was evident when we played. I would hear stories from recruits where players and coaches at other schools would tell them, "Why go to Tennessee and be a role player when you can come here and be a star?" I would just laugh it off. They had no idea that each player on our team was important, that we all had a role to play.

I was on course to graduate with my degree in political science, we were favored to win another national championship, and I would soon reach my dream of playing professional basketball. Just before the season started, we went to visit the President at the White House for the third year in a row. By then I was on a first name basis with one of the most powerful people in the world. It was unreal to me that Bill Clinton knew my name. He also knew my game and said that he was a fan of my in-and-out move. I never would have thought in my wildest dreams that I would get to have these types of experiences. I was truly blessed.

We learned before the season that we would be without our defensive superstar, Kyra Elzy, who had to have another knee surgery. That was a blow to our team, but we opened the season against Portland with a win, 94-57. We added in a triangle offense and some new defensive looks. We knew we had a tough game next at Purdue and needed to be ready. Purdue had an All-American guard, Stephanie White, and the very talented Ukari Figgs. They were a deadly pair who were true students of the game. We prepared really hard leading up to this game. We hit the floor ready to play and the game was back and forth for most of the game. They were a physical team and they were hitting on all cylinders. Our defense lacked intensity and we couldn't control the boards. It went downhill fast in the second half and they snapped our 46 game win streak. We lost, 76-68. I was upset, but I knew we would bounce back and work on our weaknesses. We were the type of team that knew how to take a game like this and learn from it. We needed to take the floor with a different attitude to avoid losing like this again. Having Tennessee across our chest made us a target every team wanted to hit.

We had a tough schedule ahead with games against Texas and Louisiana Tech coming up, but first up we had St. Joseph's, PA. We went out there and played hard hoping to get back to being "America's Hustle Team." We needed our killer instinct back and needed to ease our pain we still felt from the Purdue loss. We won easily, but we still weren't satisfied. Following the St. Joseph's game, we had twelve days without a game before we were to face Texas. So Coach gave us a few days off to heal up and get refocused.

Almost everyone headed home. I went to Chicago to spend time with Larry and his family for Thanksgiving. We had a blast as always, and I even had the chance to go watch the Chicago Condor of the now defunct American Basketball Leagues (ABL) practice. I was really excited because I had the opportunity to watch pro players like Adrienne Goodson and Yolanda Griffin. It was a great experience that motivated me to help get my team back on track. After they finished practicing, a friend introduced me to some of the team and I got a small glimpse into the future I might have. I watched as some of the players drove off in their BMWs and I wondered to myself if I would ever have a car like that.

I was really enjoying my trip. Larry took me around the city and introduced me to his family and friends. I had my first Italian Beef sandwich, some Garrett's Popcorn, and we walked by the house of Louis Farrakhan, the leader of the Nation of Islam. I have found that you can tell a lot about a person once you have been with them in their city. To get to see this side of Larry only made us closer.

While I was in Chicago, Tamika called me. She was there visiting her dad for her break. She asked me if I would mind driving back to Knoxville with her. She had to go pick up a car from her sister, who was in Champagne attending the University of Illinois. Driving back to Tennessee didn't sound like fun, but I agreed. This meant I would have to leave Larry and his family a day earlier and cancel my return ticket. The next day Larry dropped me off at Tamika's dad's condo and Tamika, her dad and I headed off to Champagne. After we picked up the car from her sister's house, we would have an additional eight hours ahead of us. We had to be back on campus at a certain time, which meant we would have to drive through the night. We agreed to split up the driving and I decided to take the first leg. It seemed like the car and time were both moving in slow motion as we drove through the small towns and cities between Chicago and Tennessee. There was nothing but headlights, white lines and darkness. The road became hypnotizing. Before I could realize it, my eyes began to shut. In the next moment I was awakened by the bumps lining the road on the shoulder. Adrenaline filled my body as I pulled the car back on the road. I could have caused a serious accident had I not woken up in time. I nudged Catch, who was asleep next to me, and woke her. I told her that I was sleepy and she needed to drive. So we switched places and I said a quick prayer and fell fast asleep. Eight hours later we arrived tired, but thankfully in one piece.

The break rejuvenated everyone, including the coaches. When we got back, Coach Summitt had some new plays and game plans to help prepare us for upcoming games. Coach worked us so hard in practice, knocking off the dust that had settled on our bodies over the break. We also watched lots of films. She wanted us to be as prepared as possible and know our opponents' every move. Our next two games would be against great teams. First up we had to face Texas, who was ranked No.2. Then on to LA Tech, both games would be on the road with a travel day in between.

The game at Texas was intense from the beginning. We walked into a packed house full of screaming fans. There wasn't an empty seat in sight and they were all there hoping to see their team take down the giants. We started that game well and held steady the entire 40 minutes. We were poised and played as a team. We did everything necessary to come out with a win, and we did just that. We had taken the first step; now it was time to get focused on LA Tech. They were that team that could really embarrass you if they gained confidence and momentum. Coach Leon Barmore had built a team of hard-nosed tough players. They rebounded the ball well, had speed, athleticism and the attitude to back it all up. It was teams like this that we would think about during the off-season while lifting weights or running sprints. We knew that when we played them we would have to be locked in from the start. They had a 52 game home winning streak one of the longest in the country at the time and I knew they would not just give us this game.

When we took the floor that game, our focus was on defense. They used their athleticism to get to the middle of the floor and to the basket. So we did our best to take away their strengths. We didn't beat them on the boards, but instead we drove the ball down their backs getting to the line 33 times and limiting them to just 12 attempts. We ended up snapping their home game win streak by beating them at their own game. I'm pretty sure their signs that read, "Welcome HBO Crybabies," gave us extra motivation.

After that win, Tech Coach Barmore threatened to step down if his team didn't improve. I knew he wasn't serious; it was just his way of motivating his team. I was happy that we were starting to look like our old selves and regaining our confidence. We didn't have any more time to waste feeling sorry for ourselves. We had to get better or let our dreams slip away. Beating these two teams was a major step in the right direction.

After that trip, Debbie Jennings, our media relations person at Tennessee, told me that I had been nominated for not one, but two ESPY awards. I was up for Women's College Basketball Player of the Year and Female Athlete of the Year. I never expected anything like that and it was amazing just to be considered. I was excited at the possibility of winning, but I knew I had to keep my focus on ball and the team.

Next, we faced University of Arkansas, our SEC rival. There was a lot of buzz about this game because I had the opportunity to break Bridgette Gordon's scoring title, 2,450. The spotlight was focused on the scoring title, but all I thought about was winning. It didn't matter if I scored a point during the next game as long as we won. The individual accolades were just a bonus for me.

Many who watched me play in college knew I wasn't much of a 3-point threat, but ironically I ended up breaking her record the first possession of the game with a 3-point shot. With that basket, I became the All Time Leading Scorer in the history of the program. Bridgette, who served as a mentor during my years at UT, was there to congratulate and present me with a plaque at half court. It was so unreal. I had become both the leading scorer and rebounder in the same year. I was most proud of the title of leading rebounder. I wouldn't let myself be denied the ball and if that meant going to the boards to get it I was more than willing.

Another highlight of my senior year was getting the opportunity to play in Madison Square Garden in front of my friends and family. It wasn't one of my better games, but we walked away with a 68-54 victory over a great Rutgers team who was coached by Hall of Famer Vivian Stringer. Rutgers had always been known for their tenacious defense and they did an amazing job limiting the play of Catch and I, but luckily Semeka and our freshman, Michelle Snow, had great games. I was so proud of Snow, who stepped in for our starting center, Teresa Geter, after she went down with a knee injury while trying to block a shot a few weeks before in the UCLA game.

From the start of the season people were talking about our lack of depth, especially after the loss to Purdue. It only got worse after losing Elzy and Geter. The training room was like a revolving door, but we had what other teams didn't: Jenny Moshak. She was our secret weapon that kept us on the court and healthy. She was a great trainer that the players trusted. She always looked out for our best interests and after putting her healing hands on Elzy and Geter, they were back in the lineup versus South Carolina. We played them before our big rival game against UConn.

We beat South Carolina by 19, but didn't play well. The tempo of the game was in their favor and we only won because they couldn't put the ball in the hole that game. We dodged a bullet as we unsuccessfully dealt with the pressure of everyone comparing us to last year's team. I was quoted as saying, "Can we blame others for comparing us to last year's team? No. We set the standard. Right now, we are just not living up to it." The media ran with my words and my team was affected by what I had said.

As we prepared to head up to Storrs, Connecticut, to face UConn, there was a lot of controversy surrounding Semeka Randall and the comments she made after the first meeting between our two teams. Every time she took the floor, Semeka played with high energy and great passion. She went hard every possession, rarely ever taking a play off. We had beat UConn last year, 84-69, and Semeka netted 25 points. In the post-game interview she commented, "I think UConn about ran off the floor, they were so scared." UConn saw the comment as disrespectful. Geno, UConn's head coach, responded by saying, "She's a little cocky. I'll admit that's one of the reasons I recruited her. But if she had any guts, she would have said it to the UConn media." We all knew after that exchange of words they would be fired up and ready to play. We knew their fans would be all over Semeka and it was going to be a huge challenge for her mentally. UConn was one of the toughest places to play in the country due to their great fan support, and with us coming to town it was sure to be a sellout crowd. We even heard rumors that tickets were being scalped for over $300. I had heard about tickets being scalped for the men's games, but never the women's. This showed just how far the women's college game had come, and that people appreciated our talent.

In a sold-out nationally televised game on CBS we defeated UConn, 92-81. Semeka played out of her mind on both ends of the floor, leading us with 26 points. The Three Meeks (Tamika, Semeka, and I) had a combined total of 68 points. I finished with 25 points and 9 boards, but sat out for long stretches on the bench with Tamika because of our foul trouble. Prior to that we were ranked No. 2 and UConn No. 1, so it was a huge win for us moving us back to the number one spot.

Playing for Tennessee meant that we were going to be the biggest draw of the year wherever we played. With that came a sense of responsibility to bring our A game every night. I'll never forget my freshman year when Coach Summitt said to me, "Mique, do you understand that everywhere we go, folks want to see if this Holdsclaw kid is the real deal?" I never let that thought leave my mind when we walked into an arena. I would motivate my teammates and myself by saying, "Hey, they're here to see us. Let's put on a great show." For the most part, we did not disappoint.

A week before our big game at LSU I was headed to attend the ESPYs at Radio City Music Hall in my hometown. I ended up winning both Female Athlete of the Year and Women's College Basketball Player of the Year. Samuel L. Jackson, who was raised in Tennessee, was the host and was aware of my team's success on the court. To open the show he threw a basketball out to me and honestly, I didn't know it was coming. Good thing I had great reflexes and quick hands otherwise I would have been hit in the face with a ball on national TV. It was an honor to be recognized among some of the best talents in sports, and having Coach Summitt and my family there only made it better.

When I got back from New York I found out that I was also the winner of the Sullivan Award. This is given to American's top amateur athlete. So many amazing things were happening to me that I often had to pinch myself. The media attention I received was intense and sometimes frightening, but it came with the territory. It was overwhelming to balance school, basketball, my personal life and this heightened attention. I appreciated all I had achieved, but I sometimes felt suffocated.

As we started to prepare for LSU, Kellie and I knew how important this game was. We seniors had never won there before and we didn't want to leave UT winless at LSU. It was our last regular season game and we wanted to go out with a bang. This game was also important because we wanted to have momentum going into the SEC tournament. Unfortunately, everything fell apart for us and we cracked under the pressure. LSU defeated us, 72-69. Our execution was horrible and our defense was even worse. I passed up on a game-winning shot as they double-teamed me at the top of the key. I knew better, but I had lost my poise and made a bad decision that cost us the game. I had won games with last second shots before but tonight I failed to rise to the challenge.

With the SEC tournament approaching we definitely had some things to fine tune. We had five days to get it together or watch all we had worked for all season long go down the drain. The LSU game sparked our mission. We returned to form and played some amazing ball. We won every game and faced Georgia in the title game, winning 85-69. We were headed back to the NCAA tournament.

Due to our success in the tournament in the previous years, ESPN picked us to be a part of their selection show. It was a big difference from the year before when we were called "America's Hustle Team" and the favorite to walk away with a NCAA Championship. This year, the tournament was considered to be wide open, with no clear-cut favorite. ESPN analyst Mimi Griffin questioned our competitive hunger and stated that in her opinion we had been "bored" during the regular season. Her comments struck a chord with some of the players and I was ready to play as soon as I heard the words leave her mouth. We were 28-2 headed into the tournament and for many, that's a great season, but because we went 39-0 the previous season, we had a lot of pressure. When you are on top, everyone is gunning for you, even the media. There was nothing we could do except lace up our sneakers and get to work. We were awarded a No.1 seed in the East Regional and would face Appalachian State in our first game. The other top teams in our region were No.2 Old Dominion, No.3 Duke and No.4 Virginia.

The SEC sent eight teams to the tournament that year and the strength of the conference was undeniable. It was the most bids that any conference had received in the tournament's 18-year history. We knew we had our work cut out for us and we talked about it often. One of the biggest gifts I've been blessed with is my ability to block everything out and focus on the task at hand (later, of course, I would realize this was also a big curse). I knew that if we stayed loose, worked hard, studied our scouting reports, and most of all, listened to Coach Summitt, we would see ourselves victorious again. It was like we were preparing for a final exam. There could be no missteps or we would find ourselves watching a new team cut down the nets and be crowned champions.

We were at our best when we played actively on defense, which led to instant offense. We didn't want teams to slow us down and force us into playing a half-court game. We weren't terrible at executing in the half court, but it allowed teams to pack it in the paint and take away our ability to get to the basket. When we were out and running, we were, so everyone said, a joy to watch.

As we approached the Appalachian State game, I will never forget my roommate Zakiah saying, "Room dog, these folks just won't give you guys a break." She was referring to an article written about us in the paper. The article said that all the media attention was a distraction. The fact that I was on the cover of *TV Guide* and had featured articles in *Newsweek* and *Time* took away from my focus on the game. They stated how our practice players had even their own feature story in *Sports Illustrated*. No other women's team received this type of press and they didn't think we could handle it. As much as they wanted us to be, we were not affected by the attention. We blocked out the buzz and went to work.

Appalachian State couldn't compete with us and we started out with a 19-0 run which led us to a 113-54 victory. We won but suffered the loss of our All-American guard, Semeka Randall, to injury. She landed on the foot of an Appalachian State player and tore ligaments in her ankle. We were all concerned because we knew how valuable she was to our team. Randall was a monster all over the court and was our defense specialist. There was no way she was going to be able to move effectively with her ankle in that condition. I'm sure Jenny Moshak, our trainer, got tired of me harassing her, asking if Randall would be okay to play. With Randall being out for the next game against Boston College, I knew we had to pick up the slack. This would be the last game I would play at the University of Tennessee, so I was very emotional. Playing in Thompson Boling arena had been the greatest experience in my life and I couldn't believe that my days playing there were about to come to an end. I was determined to leave my supporters with one great lasting impression.

I came out on fire and scored 23 first-half points. I scored at will, fueled by the crowd. I ended up tying my career high with 39 points. When Coach Summitt called her final timeout to get me off the court I ran to half court and got down on my knees and kissed the court. When I jumped up the fans gave me a standing ovation and chanted my name. When the game was finished, I rushed to the locker room. I was really happy for Kristen "Ace" Clement, who filled in for Semeka. She was ready and contributed 9 points, 9 boards and 5 assist. She took advantage of the opportunity and was ready. I must have given her at least ten hugs and told her how proud I was of her. Had it not been for her we might not have won that night. Now we were headed to Greensboro, North Carolina, for the NCAA East Regional. We played well the first round and it looked like we were on pace to repeat as champions.

After our games, Tennessee hosted NCAA games on the men's side. So before we headed out, Kellie and I decided to go watch the University of Maryland men's team practice. They were having a great season led by NBA prospect and junior college transfer Steve Francis. A few minutes into watching their practice Kellie leaned over and asked, "Mique, why does Steve Francis keep looking up here at you? Do you guys know each other?" I told her no and brushed it off. She said, "Mique, really, he just keeps looking." I told her no again and continued to watch. I loved watching other teams to see how they prepared for games.

Our first game of the East Regional was against Virginia Tech. We found out just before we left that Semeka was healing fast and would be back in uniform to play. It was spring break and she and Jenny Moshak were able to spend a lot of time together in the training room getting her healthy. During the Virginia Tech game, her energy and charisma gave us a boost. She didn't play as many minutes as she usually did, but she displayed tremendous heart and gave us what she could. We won and were now preparing to face Duke, who had defeated Old Dominion earlier that day.

Duke was a really scrappy team that we defeated in the regular season, 74-60, at a tournament in Orlando. They were lead by 6'6 center, Michelle Van Gorp, and guard Hilary Howard. Howard was from New York and was a former AAU teammate of mine so I knew of her abilities. We were definitely going to be in for a good game. Duke was peaking at the right time, playing their best basketball of the season. In the media, the Duke team played into their role as the underdog. I knew that player-for-player they could not handle us. We were too athletic and explosive, so I knew they would have a trick up their sleeves. They would be well prepared with a definitive game plan of how to stop us.

From the tip it was clear that they were very prepared. They took away our strengths and played aggressively. They were poised on offense, took good shots and played as a team. The roles were reversed that day, and we looked like the underdogs. Our worst nightmare was coming true as the clock ticked down. Each second that passed we saw our dream of repeating as national champions slip through our fingers. Everything that could go wrong that day did. Duke pulled off what was probably the biggest upset in their program's history, defeating us 68-52.

Duke executed their game plan perfectly. They had their best defense player, Peppi Browne, chase me around the whole night. She face guarded me every play and when I did get the ball, she forced me to take a set jump shot, which wasn't a strong part of my game. I had played perfectly into her hand; she encouraged me to play outside of my strengths and exposed my weaknesses. I shot a dismal 2-18 from the floor.

On top of my poor performance, Catch got into early foul trouble with two fouls at the start of the game. We had trouble scoring and we allowed that to affect our defense and rebounding. Prior to the Duke's game I averaged 28.3 points per game in the tournament but walked away with just 8 that night. At the half I pleaded with Semeka, telling her that we needed her more than ever that night. We were playing terribly. She said, "Mique, I'm trying baby, but my ankle is killing me." I knew she was giving all she could, but I could see the game slipping away from us.

And thus my storybook career at Tennessee was over. As I fouled out I went to the sideline in tears. I hugged Coach Summitt then walked to the end of the bench and buried my face in my hands. I was in total shock. Once the buzzer sounded my heart sank. My time playing in a Lady Vol uniform was officially over.

When we got back to the locker room I sat in my locker in the corner with a towel over my head and sobbed. I couldn't believe what had just happened. Minutes later Coach Summitt came over and told me, "Mique, keep your head up. I'm so proud of you and what you have done for this program. You have nothing to be ashamed of. You have to handle your failures just as you would your success." Not only did we lose, but I had played the worst game of the season. But encouraged by my coach's words I wiped the tears from my face and thought about how blessed I was to have been able to play for such an incredible woman. From that moment on I never shed another tear. When I finally left the locker room, I walked into the arms of my fiancé Larry and he consoled me. It was comforting to know that he was there for me. Without the support of the people who loved me, I don't know how I would have left that locker room that day. When we arrived back to Knoxville our fans were there to support us. Some fans even left flowers and cards at my apartment. Former UT standout, Peyton Manning, even gave me a call to wish me the best and to let me know he was proud of me.

The sting of losing was hard to swallow, but I had to prepare to head to San Jose, California, to play in the Women's Basketball Coaches Association all-star game with Kellie. Tamika, Semeka, and I were also named

Kodak All-Americans, so we had to attend a presentation. I was also going to be honored as the Associated Press Player of the Year, and my family was going to be there. Since everyone had expected us to make it back to the Final Four, my family had their tickets and planned a family gathering with my cousins out west in Havre, Montana. I had the chance to spend the weekend with my cousins, Thurman Jr. and Kassala, the children of my late Uncle TJ. I remember my Aunt Stacey asking me how I dealt with the media and fans wanting my autograph. I told her that it was just a part of the game and that I appreciated all the people who came out and supported my team and me every night. It's hard to imagine now that in college I appeared in nearly 700 interviews and photo shoots in my senior year alone.

I received a phone call from a good friend of mine saying that he knew someone he wanted me to meet and possibly date. I had to decline his offer. Several people had tried to hook me up with their friends, but I was in a relationship and I valued that. I remember one of my guy friends from New York had tried to hook me up with former NFL running back Sedrick Irvin. Sedrick and I had hung out a few times when he was in New York visiting family the year before my senior season. We ended up being good friends because I truly loved and cared for Larry. Still, I got letters and pictures from all types of guys, including pro athletes. They would send me their phone numbers, but I just wasn't interested.

I remember talking to Michael Bivins of New Edition about it. Since he had first contacted me during my freshman year, we had remained in touch. He told me how it was in the industry, and that when you are hot everyone wants a piece of you. He then went to talk about the Brat and even though her image was one of a tomboy, she was still a beautiful woman. She was, as he stated, the "hottest in the game" and everyone was trying to get at her.

When I arrived back in Knoxville, things moved at a frantic pace. I met with Coach Summitt so we could decide on an agent. My eligibility was up, so my phone was ringing off the hook with calls from agents and runners. I had no clue how they got my number or who I could trust. I was solicited with incredible offers and I wasn't sure who to go with. Entertainers were trying to break into the business during this time. Rapper Master P had started a sports company and was trying to make his mark in the world of sports. You can only imagine as a college kid how overwhelming it was receiving calls from Queen Latifah, Master P, and Sean Diddy Combs' people. Pat sat down with me and we went through several packets of prospective agents and decided on three. Next we set up meetings so that I could meet them face-to-face and hear their future plans for me.

The WNBA had already held their lottery and it was predicted I would be the No.1 draft pick and head to Washington, DC to play for the Washington Mystics. I was excited about that possibility because that meant I would be closer to home. Still, I couldn't get too excited with the ABL seizing operations. It meant that all of those players were now available for the WNBA Draft.

The meeting with the agents and attorneys went well. I met with firms from Chicago, DC, and NY. I didn't make a rushed decision and took my time. One of my friends who played ball connected me with a guy from New York who was more involved with the entertainment industry. He was young and fun, but smart about his business. We hit if off immediately. I loved his energy and could appreciate that he was a hustler. After several phone conversations, I told him come to Knoxville for a meeting. I realized his gift was marketing and his ideas were great. I was conflicted and gave myself a week to make a decision. I loved the cooperate appeal of some of the other companies, but admired the creativity and enthusiasm of the agent I'd met from New York.

I called my grandma and asked her to pray on my decision. She told me that people were calling her house everyday trying to get a hold of me. About a week later, I decided to sign with the young agent from New York. We started to make plans so I told Coach Summitt. She loved his energy, but didn't think he would be great on the contractual side. He didn't have any experience. I took all she said into account and I decided to have William & Connolly Law Firm represent me. The head of the sports department and partner in the firm was Lon Babby. Working with him was attorney Jim Tanner. They also represented Tim Duncan and Grant Hill in the NBA. It was agreed they would represent me, but the agent from New York would do my marketing.

Now that the hard part of finding an agent was over, I could just focus on basketball. Prior to the WNBA draft I worked out with assistant Coach Al Brown around my classes to stay sharp and in shape. I made the most of the time left at school. I was going to miss all the people who made my time here unforgettable, people like my friend, Eli, who was a political science major. He always looked out for me and made sure I had the notes I needed for class when we would travel. As a token of my appreciation, I gave him my Tennessee letterman jacket. He was so shocked and questioned me: "Mique, are you kidding?" I told him no and that I wanted to thank him for always being such a great friend. I could have not made it through my major had it not been for his great friendship.

In the weeks that led up to the draft I received a call from Lon wanting to discuss some business. He told me that I had a few shoe companies—Adidas, Nike, and Reebok— interested in signing me. I jumped for joy and asked him to set up meetings. A week later Larry and I were on a first class flight from Knoxville, TN to Portland, Oregon. I was so glad he was able to come with me because things were happening fast. He was the calm in my life amidst the chaos. When we arrived there was a limo waiting for us and we were taken to the hotel. My mouth dropped as we walked into our hotel suite. I had only seen rooms like this in movies or in magazines. Here I was, a kid from the projects living her dream.

Larry and I ate dinner that evening with Nike representative, Raye Pond, and enjoyed a casual stroll around the city before calling it a night. The following morning Lon asked me a question, "How much are you looking to make yearly in this deal?" I really had no clue what I should ask for. I had heard some figure thrown out there in the streets and by other agents, so I just threw him a high six figure amount. He looked at me like I was crazy. He said that he didn't think it was realistic. I asked him what was realistic and he replied with a much lower six-figure number. I told him that I disagreed. He went on to explain how one of his female clients had the largest shoe deal for a women's basketball player with Fila. He was well aware of what was realistic and what wasn't. He was the pro in this arena and all of this business negotiating was new for me. I told him to just get me the best deal possible. I then headed upstairs to get my stuff.

Larry and I then met up with Raye Pond again and drove through town in a limo. I was caught off guard when we pulled up; there, outstretched over the entrance to the campus was a big banner that read "Welcome Chamique." Everyone was wearing "Welcome Chamique" T-shirts. I was shocked that they had put so much effort into making me feel welcome. I got a tour of Nike's campus and it was phenomenal. I had a chance to meet the shoe designers and learn the science behind making a shoe. I met with all of the executives and then went shopping at the Nike Employee store. I was like a kid in a candy store as I shopped for friends, my family and myself.

We then headed to meet with the Co-Founder of Nike, Phil Knight. I was in awe of meeting one of the men responsible for creating such an amazing company. Once we were finished, we headed back to the hotel. Lon and I sat down for a conversation. He said, "I have to tell you something, Mique. I really underestimate the value of the contract. The numbers they threw out were more than I had imagined and more towards your end of things." When he repeated the figures all I could do was smile and think about being able to help my family move out of the projects.

The next morning Larry and I headed back to Knoxville. A few days later Lon called me letting me know that he had set up a meeting with Adidas, but the rep wanted to come to meet me in Knoxville. A few days later I was in Coach Summitt's office sitting down, talking with the Adidas rep. He told me he was impressed with my talent, but he wanted to make sure I wanted to wear Adidas. He asked me questions like who was my best friend, what were my favorite colors, what did I like about Adidas. His approach was a little unorthodox, but I understood where he was coming from. Adidas was appealing because at the time they didn't have any other female basketball players, whereas Nike had several. He said he didn't want a bidding war and the back and forth. If I wanted to sign with Adidas, he said just to tell him right *now*. Honestly, he lost me on that because I was going after the overall best deal. Secondly, I couldn't make a decision without my agent. The meeting finally came to an end and he said he would be in contact with my agent.

I had no one to talk to outside of Lon and Jim. I didn't feel comfortable about talking with any of my friends or family about money. I had to grow up and make some difficult decisions. After the meeting with Adidas I got a call from my marketing guy saying that he had been in discussion with Reebok. He went over the package with me. It was by far the most lucrative, but I had to look past the dollar amount and consider what the brand stood for. Plus, I had to want to wear the product. Nike reflected my style the most, I would be Adidas' only female athlete, and Reebok's deal was the most lucrative. These were all things I needed to consider before making a final decision.

Lon called later that week to tell me the Adidas package was nowhere near Nike's overall so I took them off the list. I then removed Reebok I hadn't worn their shoes since eigth grade and didn't see myself playing in them. I told Lon my final decision so he went back and forth with Nike on some details over the next few days. Once things were finalized I called Raye Pond and told her I was joining the Nike family. After everything was signed and finalized I went home to my apartment, dropped down to my knees, and just started crying. I was beyond grateful and I knew from that point on my life would be different. I had just signed a multimillion-dollar contract. I was going to be able to buy a house in a safe neighborhood. I could help show my family a better life. And before I could take all of this in and wipe the tears from my face the marketing guys called to tell me a deal with Nickelodeon was on the table for two years. He told me the terms and I agreed. Nickelodeon signed me as a special sports correspondent for the Nickelodeon Games & Sports cable network. I could not believe how drastically my life was changing.

Before I could catch my breath I was off to LA to be a presenter at the Nickelodeon Kid's Choice Awards. After that I would have to head to New York for the WNBA Draft. Once I arrived and got settled, the marketing rep took me for a tour of the city. I laughed to myself as I strolled down world famous Rodeo Drive. It was a far cry from the projects I called home.

The next day was the Kid's Choice Awards. I got my makeup done in the same trailer as Bill Bellamy and Sporty Spice of the Spice Girls. After makeup I went to the green room to wait with the rest of the talent. There I met LL Cool J, who was a Queens native, and T-Boz from TLC I even got a picture with Justin Timberlake and Chris Tucker. I was among some of Hollywood's elite and it was incredible.

After the awards I flew to New York for the draft. May 4th was the day I had thought about often throughout my life and it had finally come. I called my grandmother the morning before the draft crying. I said to her, "Grandma, do you remember how I used to write all of those letters saying I was going to be a professional basketball player, I was going to be the first girl to play in the NBA?" Of course she remembered. She told me how proud she was and how my dream would come true today. She said, "No matter what, Chamique, just keep that good heart you have. Don't change, just remain humble." She went on to tell me how she prayed so much for me and how she prayed me into this position. She talked about all the hard times we had gone through when I came to live with her and how God had changed my life. She said, "I was on my knees everyday asking God to look over you, Chamique. He is using you, just remember that." When I got off the phone with her I flopped down on my bed in the hotel room and stared at the ceiling, thinking of my future.

My grandmother met me a few hours later at the draft. It was just as much her draft day as it was mine. She had groomed me and watched me grow. She lived every second of my dream with me and I wanted her there.

I was full of pride as I heard my name called. I was officially the No.1 pick of the 1999 draft, headed to the Washington Mystics. I could see tears of joy running down my grandmother's face as she heard my name. I hugged her and walked to the podium full of hope. All I ever wanted was to make my grandmother proud, and I had done all of that and more. The following day I flew to DC to do some press and meet the coaches and everyone who worked in the front office for the organization. Abe Pollin owned the Mystics he also owned the NBA team, the Washington Wizards.

When I arrived, I met Susan O'Malley, the president of our team. She had been a part of history in her own right. Susan was the first female president of an NBA franchise, and at the young age of 29. Her energy and charisma were contagious. After that meeting I headed to meet our General Manager, Wes Unseld, who was an NBA Hall of Famer. They welcomed me to DC and let me know that they were there to make my transition a smooth one. Once I had met everyone I then headed down to Union Station where there was a Washington Mystics celebration welcoming me. I was overwhelmed by the big turnout. They had DC radio personality Big Tigger, of WPGC 95.5, who was also a New Yorker, emceeing the event. I was like a big kid with wide eyes. I felt so welcomed and excited to begin a new chapter. I went back to my hotel and caught up with my high school teammate Kristeena. She happened to be a student at George Washington University in DC. She said, "See Mique, I told you this city would love you. You have to remember that DC is a sports town." She was right; I felt supported by the fans before I had even taken a jump shot.

The next day I met with a real estate agent to find a place to live. That day she showed me five houses. They were beautiful, but I didn't want a house that would be too big, so she suggested a townhouse. Finally, I decided that I should just rent for a year until I was more familiar with the area. Lon and I conveyed that to the agent, and she showed us some rentals. I narrowed it down to two homes and called Sashia, our team's community relations person, to look at them and to see if they were in an area that was safe. She came and helped me make the final choice.

Once I finished that process I headed over to my agent Jim Tanner's house for dinner. It was comforting to know he lived just five minutes from the property I selected. After dinner, I met back up with my former high school teammate. We hung out all night in my hotel room reminiscing about our days in high school. The next morning I went to the airport to head back to Knoxville to finish packing and enjoy the rest of my time there before graduation. While waiting at the airport I had to give former UConn star, Rita Williams, a phone call. Raye Pond from Nike reminded me to call Rita to see if she would give up her No.23 for me. When I asked General Manager Wes Unseld about the number, he said it was something that I had to work out with Rita. I remember when I called I was so nervous. I said, "Hey Rita, this is Chamique..." and I started off the conversation with some small talk. Rita then sighed and said, "Chamique, I know what you are calling about." I offered to pay her or buy her a watch. She said she wouldn't accept money, but that I could get her something. At the end of the conversation she agreed to let me have the number. I made sure my agent told the Mystics and I called Raye to tell her the good news. It wasn't so much the number, but the meaning behind the number that meant so much.

When I arrived back to Knoxville, Larry met me at the airport. It had been an eventful, life-changing week and I wanted to share every detail with him. That day we decided that he would join me in DC once he finished his obligations at work. I could not see myself starting this new chapter in my life without him.

Soon after my return to Knoxville I received a call from my agents telling me I had to report to training camp by May 16. They were firm on this and I would be fined if I reported late. I was to be a bridesmaid in Kellie Jolly's wedding on the fifteenth so I had to figure out a way to be in the wedding *and* arrive on time to camp. So I asked my good friend Shawn to drive to DC with me after Kellie's wedding. I said that I would pay for her to fly back to Knoxville if she would help me. Thankfully, she agreed.

I had just a few days left before graduation and the wedding. I spent my time saying goodbye to the many people who had looked after and supported me during my time in Knoxville. The day before graduation, my grandmother and father arrived. I was so happy that they were going to get to see me walk across the stage. I was happy to see my dad looking and feeling like a different person. The medication he was on was working and the father I had always loved was reemerging. I was happy to have them there, but also sad that my mom couldn't put the past behind her and attend. She didn't want to be around my father. I was disappointed, but having my father and grandmother there was plenty.

On May 14, 1999, I became the first person in my immediate family to graduate from college. It was an amazing feeling to hear my name read as I walked across the stage. When I was handed that paper I held it up in my hand until I got across the stage. I was happy I could give my grandmother the only thing she had ever asked of me. After the graduation ceremony, I headed to the Lady Vol locker room and signed my name on our famous graduation pole. I wanted to celebrate with Larry and my family, but was unable to do so because I had committed to attend Kellie's wedding rehearsal. Thankfully, Zakiah agreed to take my place and fill in as hostess to my family. I hugged my dad, my grandmother, and my coaches and kissed Larry goodbye as I headed to Sparta, Tennessee for Kellie's wedding. I wasn't sure what was ahead of me, but I was excited for whatever life brought next.

FOURTH QUARTER

CHAPTER 13

New Beginnings

I was filled with emotions as I prepared for this new chapter of my life. My mind raced as I wondered what things were going to be like on my new team. I was nervous about the unknown. I wondered if I would fit in with these women and if we would be successful. In an effort to quiet my thoughts, I familiarized myself with the training camp roster. I thought if I knew more about each player I would be better prepared and less nervous.

The morning of our first practice I received a knock on my door from Markita Aldridge. Markita was from Detroit and had played at UNC Charlotte. She wanted to let me know I could ride with her to practice or follow her. To ease my butterflies I decided to ride with her and a few other girls to practice. When we arrived at the MCI Center we headed to the locker room to get ready for practice. I found the locker with the No.23 attached to it, walked over, sat down and took a deep breath. I knew that locker and we would spend a lot of time together. Moments later in walked Nikki McCray, the star of the franchise and fellow Tennessee Lady Vol. Nikki had a magnetic personality and she made me feel comfortable right away.

Once everyone got taped and ready, the coaches walked in and welcomed us. They told us what the first practice would consist of and encouraged each of us to relax, have fun and do our best. The head coach was Nancy Darsch, and our assistant coach was Melissa McFerrin. They had been coaching together for several years and had been very successful at Ohio State University. After our brief meeting, we headed to the court to start practice. Our trainer warmed us up and we stretched together as a team. We then started with full court passing drills to get our bodies going. Practice was intense and there was a clear increase in the speed of the game and overall athleticism of the players from what I had known in college. On the first play I got my shot blocked by Penny Moore, who was from the DC area and was a veteran after playing many years overseas. It was a wake up call that I received loud and clear. This was not college anymore and I was going to have to really work on my fakes and timing if I was going to succeed at this level.

After practice the coaches asked me how I felt and if I was getting adjusted. I told them that it had been a long three days and that I was tired. I was then pulled away and asked to speak to the media. There were about ten reporters waiting for me who wanted to know how my first practice went. I told them how things went well and how I was excited to help the team in anyway I could.

We left the gym and the girls and I decided to go to lunch. On our way there, Rita told me she decided what she wanted in return for her giving me her number. I held my breath as she spoke. I just knew she was going to ask for something outrageous. She said that she wanted some golf clubs. I exhaled a sigh of relief and told her that I would get them to her as soon as possible. I sent Raye Pond, my Nike rep, a message and asked if she could get Rita the clubs. Golf had become popular among the African American community due to the success of Tiger Woods. For lunch, my teammates selected a restaurant that served Chinese, soul food, and sandwiches. It was an interesting combination to say the least. I quickly grabbed something to eat and headed back to the hotel. I needed to get some rest before my second practice that night.

In order to be as prepared as possible, our coaches had us practice twice a day. It was difficult to get used to and left my body sore. Every day we worked on executing the coaches' playing philosophy. We worked tirelessly to find our identity as a team. I was on the phone every night complaining to Larry about how tired my body was. After helping me get settled, my friend Shawn headed back to Knoxville. I really appreciated her being there with me those first few days. The transition wasn't easy and it was comforting to have a friendly face around.

With each day that passed I got a better feel for the professional game. The coaches did a nice job of easing me in so that I didn't feel any pressure, but I knew once the lights came on many would accept nothing but greatness from me. My teammates did all they could to help me get adjusted on the court, but Rita Williams and I connected the most. She gave me advice about playing at this level and shared what she had learned the previous year playing in the WNBA. She was also from the East Coast and graduated from a top program UConn where she played for Geno. We had a lot in common and quickly became good friends.

One day after practice, Sashia called me and told me that a good friend of hers wanted to meet me. She told me that Steve Francis had been bugging her about meeting me ever since I had been drafted there. She then asked if it was okay for her to give him my phone number. Most of my friends were guys so I thought nothing of it and told her it was fine. I thought it would be nice to have someone show me around the DC metro area. Later that evening, Steve called and we talked for about 20 minutes. He congratulated me on my success and told me that he liked my game. He said if I needed anything to call him and that he would check up on me from time to time to make sure I was doing well.

"From time to time" turned into the next day. He called and asked if I would like to get something to eat after practice. Starved for a good meal, I agreed. He picked me up from the hotel and I noticed we had the same car, in the same color. As we talked more and more, we realized we had many things in common. The greatest thing we had in common was that our grandmothers had raised us both. Steve's mom had passed away from cancer and his dad was alive but dealing with his own issues. We shared stories of our youth and talked about our experiences playing basketball.

I felt like I was talking to the male version of myself. That night at Ruth's Chris Steakhouse on Wisconsin Avenue in Bethesda, a friendship was born. We laughed and argued about a bunch of things, but our true passion came out when we went back and forth about who had the best players, New York or DC. I laughed and told him that if DC wanted to even compete with New York, he would have to include players from Virginia and Maryland too. I argued that we would blow them out the park with our bench players. This type of banter continued for most of the night. It felt like talking to one of my childhood friends.

Practice got better and I was having such a good experience. My confidence grew with each practice and so did the team's. I was having fun learning with my teammates and was excited for the journey ahead. The Mystics led the league in attendance the previous season, and so I knew we would have the fan support needed to turn things around.

A week and a half into training camp I was handed the keys to my new house. I had no furniture yet, but I was happy to have a space that was my own. I walked into my new home for the first time and sat on the floor and sobbed. Not so long ago I had called the walls of a project apartment home and now I had more space than I knew what to do with. I thought back to the day when my hand was burned during my baptismal. Maybe God *had* anointed my hands that day. I also thought of my grandmother's words to me before I left for college, about how once I graduated, I couldn't come home. Now I walked through my new home and looked forward to all the memories I would make within these walls.

After some time alone in the house I drove back to the hotel. I would have to stay there a few more days until my furniture arrived. On the way there I called Larry to share what I was feeling. I told him how much I was looking forward to him coming to DC and assured him that he would love the city. I couldn't wait to introduce him to all the new people I had met. Larry planned to come to DC after our preseason game in Tennessee and we both counted down the days.

About halfway through camp the coaches cut down practice to once a day. We scrimmaged most of the practice, trying to simulate what it was going to be like during a game. The coaches looked at different combinations of players and tried to determine who played well together. I was focused. We were headed to Knoxville in a week to play against the Houston Comets in a preseason game. I was going to be making my WNBA debut in front of the fans that supported and loved me. The WNBA started its first season in 1997, which was my sophomore year at Tennessee. I was so excited when the league first started because it would give the opportunity to play pro basketball in the USA. The Comets had some amazing players on their team. Cynthia Cooper, Sheryl Swoopes, Tina Thompson, and Janeth Arcain had led the team to back-to-back championship and were favored to repeat as such. I was eager to see how our team stacked up against the world's best.

My furniture arrived a few days before we were set to leave for Knoxville and it felt amazing to be finally living in my house and sleeping in my own bed. Outside of practice I was enjoying getting used to my surroundings. The day after my furniture came Steve Francis, who was free from pre-draft workouts, called and asked me to meet him downtown. I told him he could pick me up from the arena after my practice. We went down to S.W DC near the Wharf and ate fish sandwiches. After we finished, he took me to meet his family. I met his grandmother, Mrs. Wilson, his brother Terry and his sister Tiffany. We sat around talking and laughing for hours before heading back to the arena. On the drive home he said it was so hard for him to decide what girls where real and which ones were interested in him just because of who he was. He was going through some tough times with his ex-girlfriend and wasn't sure what he wanted to do. I told him to just try his best to avoid the girls who seemed like they just wanted to be with him for the money. I went on to tell him how excited I was that Larry was finally coming to DC. He joked about not being able to hang with me anymore once he arrived. I laughed it off and told him we could still be friends.

Before I knew it, my new team was headed to Knoxville. Thompson

Boling Arena was my home and I couldn't wait to get back to my comfort zone. I felt prepared and I wanted to give the fans a good show. We arrived early and headed to the festivities surrounding the opening of the new Women's Basketball Hall of Fame. I was told I would be receiving an award, but I was shocked when the Knoxville City Council officially dedicated Chamique Holdsclaw Drive to me. Immediately I knew Coach Summitt had fought for this one. At the ceremony she told me "Mique, you deserve this because you have done so much for this University." Chamique Holdsclaw Drive runs, very appropriately, into Thompson Boling Arena.

The next day in our exhibition game we defeated the Houston Comets 68-64. I dropped in 20 points, collected 10 rebounds and dished 6 assists to help my team win. I was glad the fans were able to see a great game. I felt the preseason games gave people a glimpse of what to expect during the regular season. After my performance I knew that players were going to come after me hard on the defensive end. I would be the focus of every team we would face that summer. *The Washington Post* even ran a story about what my impact might mean for the WNBA. They discussed my skill, my endorsements, and they compared me to the many greats before me. It was an honor to be viewed with such great regard. I took the responsibility of being paid such a great compliment seriously.

We had good momentum heading into our season opener at the MCI Center. The arena was packed. It was inspiring to see the sea of Holdsclaw jerseys worn by fans. I was also pleased to see my grandmother and friends in the crowd supporting me. I heard my name announced in the starting line up, then we took the floor and battled with an experienced Charlotte team. After several lead changes we lost a close game to the Sting, 73-83. I was disappointed but didn't have time to sulk: we were flying out in the morning to face the Houston Comets. We were confident about our chances against this team especially since we beat them in the preseason. It was going to be my first nationally televised game since coming to the WNBA. I wanted to do my best to make sure my television debut went off without a hitch, so I made sure to get a good rest the night before the game.

My team and I were focused as we took the floor that night, but it was clear from the beginning that we were no match for the defending champs. We came off like a college team against them as they defeated us 63-88. Sheryl Swoopes guarded me tightly the whole night and shut me out of the game. She locked in on me from the beginning and would not let me put on a show like I had when we played them in Knoxville. On the defensive end, it seemed impossible to shut down their big three. Swoopes, Cooper, and Thompson looked unstoppable. I was held to just 6 points on 3 of 14 shooting. I did, however, have 13 rebounds. Receiving their championship rings in the ceremony before the game and being on national TV definitely motivated them that night. They were clearly the better team while we were still trying to find our way.

After the game the coaches briefly talked to us about the game. They encouraged us to keep working hard and said if we did things would improve. The locker room was then opened to the media for questioning. My locker was soon surrounded by reporters asking me questions about the game and my adjustment to the WNBA. One reporter approached me asking me to comment on what Sheryl had to say after the game. I was livid about the comments he said she made about me after the game. He told me how she was tired of hearing and reading about me and that it wasn't my fault, but I was the target right now. I wanted to respond to what she said, but thought it was better not to. I knew I couldn't let anyone see me sweat so when he tried to hype it up I just let it go. Markita Aldridge and Rita Williams came over to my locker after overhearing and told me I had said the right thing. As a New Yorker, I have a quick tongue and I'm always careful about saying something I might later regret.

After we finished up with the media, we headed back to the hotel. When we arrived back I went up to my room and called Larry. He told me not to be down about the game and assured me that we would get better. I was happy that he would finally be joining me in DC after our game against the NY Liberty. I really needed him, especially since things had started off so poorly for my team.

The next morning we headed to New York. I was happy to be returning to the city that raised me. After starting the season out 0-2, I was really looking for a win in my hometown. New York was a great team led by veterans Teresa Weatherspoon, Kym Hampton, and Sue Wicks. I had a history in college of not playing my best games in Madison Square Garden and really wanted to change that. I wanted to forget those memories and start building new ones, starting, of course, with a win. Playing in Madison Square Garden is a dream of every kid who has ever played basketball in New York. It's like playing on a big stage. It isn't the nicest sports arena I've ever played in, but it is the most historical and definitely the most famous.

As soon as I hit the court for pregame warm up my supporters asked for autographs and pictures. I humbly obliged, then hit the court to get locked in mentally for the game. Just before game time, Coach Darsch went over the plan one last time before we headed out to warm up. Chills rolled down my back when I heard my name announced, "Starting at forward from Astoria, N.Y No.23, Chamique Holdsclaw!" The crowd erupted and cheered for me as I walked to the free throw line to join my teammates. During our first two games, our offense had been erratic and our defense nonexistent. Tonight was much different: our defense was intense and everything flowed for us offensively. I will never forget Coach Darsch's excitement every time we came to the bench. I knew as the former head coach of the Liberty she wanted to come in and get a win. We ended up winning 83-61. I played tough on both ends of the floor and put up 20 points and grabbed 9 rebounds. I was elated that I had finally broken my streak of bad games in the Garden. After the game I was greeted with congratulatory remarks and hugs from my family and friends. Our win was a perfect way to cap off my trip home.

We arrived back to DC early the next morning. I went home for a few hours and then it was back to the airport for me to pick up Larry. I looked forward to our talks and spending my nights at my new home in his arms. There was so much I wanted to share with him. I was really excited when he finally was able to meet my teammates and put faces with names. He was my "make believe boyfriend" no longer. He was finally there in the flesh. Prior to his arrival I spent my nights with my teammates and new friends I'd made since coming to DC. I had developed my own little group of people I hung out with outside of basketball. My new circle of friends helped keep things in perspective and kept my mind from always being on basketball.

I'm not sure Larry ever thought about how hard this adjustment had been for me. I had been a winner all throughout my career and now had to adjust to life on the bottom. My head spun as I tried to think of ways to help make us better as a team. I often questioned if I was doing enough. The season was just beginning, but I was worried about how well we were going to do. I was used to winning. I had won four state championships at Christ the King, three out of four NCAA titles at Tennessee and now we were in a three-game skid and 1-5. All I could do was play hard and try to be a good teammate.

I took out my frustration on the court on Larry. When I was home with him I was moody and mean. I began to pressure him about what he was going to do for work and had very little patience with him. I didn't realize what I was doing to him and our relationship. We started bickering all the time about nothing. The smallest things agitated me and I would say things I didn't mean. My home life was becoming just as chaotic as things were on the court. I found myself happy to go to practice just to get away from the fighting. I knew I loved Larry, but I was questioning if I was just with him because I was comfortable. It broke my heart to feel this way.

When I would come home at the end of the day, I was annoyed with him being there. I felt like he wasn't contributing to building our life together and I started to feel like I was taking care of him. I didn't know how to support him and it caused a strain in our relationship. Looking back I wish I would have known patience. I didn't want to lose my relationship, so to help alleviate the negative feelings I spent more time away from home and with my teammates. Larry, of course, noticed my distance and confronted me about it. He thought I spent too much time with my new friends and not enough time with him. I didn't respond well to that and asked him to sleep in the guest bedroom because I needed my space. He agreed but in the middle of the night he found his way back into our bed and I woke up in his arms. He apologized, but it should have been me doing the apologizing. We were mutually making our relationship difficult. Nothing was ever resolved, we just swept it under the rug.

Like everyone else in the city, I focused on the excitement in DC around the approaching NBA Draft. I hadn't seen Steve Francis in a few weeks but we talked often. I was excited for him, as well as my childhood friends who were projected to be top picks in this year's draft. I followed the chatter of the media closely. And I was concerned when a usually upbeat Steve called me sounding down. I asked what was going on. He said it was predicted that Elton Brand would be drafted No.1 to Chicago and that meant that he would be drafted No.2 to Vancouver. I didn't understand why it mattered where he went; he was about to live his dream and play in the NBA. I did my best to be a good friend and listen to his concerns, but I just couldn't understand what the big deal was. The NBA is the NBA no matter where you're playing. I knew a hundred guys who would kill for a chance like this and here he was complaining about it. A few days later we were set to play Houston again. Coach Darsch went through the scouting report, detailing all of their plays and tendencies. We watched a video of our previous game and broke down the game by quarters. She told us that we were going to have to move the ball a lot better and that this team was not just a two-man show. She was referring to Nikki McCray and me. I definitely understood that and respected what she had to say. We needed to play better as a team on both ends of the floor. It seemed like we all understood what she wanted from us, but when we went out on the floor we could not produce a different result. That night we lost our fourth game in a row. Houston beat us in a close one, 69-72. I was extremely upset and emotional after the game. I had lost more games in my few short weeks as a WNBA player than I had in the last two years at UT. Losing was hard for me to swallow. After the game, Larry drove me home to pack. We had to play in Cleveland the following night.

The next morning at the airport I told Rita about how losing was becoming too much and was starting to affect my relationship with Larry. I told her that I couldn't figure out why I had been so tough on him or where these feelings were coming from. I knew part of it was that I wasn't in Knoxville anymore. I was back in the big city and there was a lot of activity. I felt like I had remained the same and thought it was the people around me who had in fact changed. My distant relatives who I'd never had a relationship with all of a sudden wanted to get closer to me. What hurt the most was when a childhood friend called and asked me to pay his college tuition and when I said that I couldn't he got angry. So many people had their hands out and wanted a piece of me. It was clear that I was no longer under that protective umbrella of Pat Summitt and the University of Tennessee. I was in the real world now with more responsibility and more burdens.

That morning in the airport I poured my heart out to Rita and she sat there and patiently listened. At the end of our conversation she asked if I loved Larry. I said yes without hesitation. She said, "Well then, try harder." I took her words into consideration and I agreed to give it my best shot.

But the trip to Cleveland did not prove to be successful for us. We suffered another loss and headed back to DC. I was exhausted. Not only did the pace of the game and the athleticism change, but so did the travel. There was no more flying on comfortable private school planes. I was now flying from game to game on commercial flights. Flying this way made back-to-back games extremely difficult to win. Having to compete the night before, then wake up early the next day to fly to the next city, and then try to get some rest before taking the court that night was a lot harder than I thought it was going to be.

I could not wait to get home to rest in my own bed. I wanted nothing more than to forget the previous night's game and sleep. However, as soon as I walked through the door I knew I wouldn't be getting any rest.

I had asked Larry to put together a TV stand and I couldn't understand why it wasn't done, when he had nothing else to do. We found ourselves bickering back and forth once again I was too tired for this so I went up to our bedroom to sleep. When I woke up a few hours later Larry was right there next to me watching television, as if we had not just fought a few hours before. He told me he had spoken to some people he knew and he was looking into a new job opportunity. I was happy for him and hoped a job would pan out for him. We talked about his plans to go to Chicago to see his family. At first I said I didn't want him to go, but then I reconsidered and reminded myself that it can't always be about me and what I want. So we agreed that he would go to Chicago for a few weeks to be with his family.

On my way to practice the next day I received a call from Steve. He wanted to know if I would go and celebrate with him after the draft. I told him I wouldn't be able to make it because we had a game in Charlotte and that I couldn't even watch the draft because I would be playing while it was going on. He sounded disappointed, but said he would call me and we would celebrate when I got back. Since we had been introduced, we probably talked to each other every day. Our relationship was fun and easy and just what I needed to help with the other stresses in my life; plus, we were going through similar challenges.

What I didn't know was that our friendship was starting to cause tension in my relationship with Larry. In a calm voice over lunch, Larry looked me in my eyes and questioned, "Chamique, are you and Steve Francis dating?" I said no, of course, and was confused; I had always had friendships with guys, and I didn't see how this friendship was any different. I was caught off guard by his allegation and his mistrust saddened me. I don't know what I would have done without basketball during this time. We weren't having the success any of us wanted on the court, but it was still there as a way to vent my frustrations. Just as it was for me as a child, basketball has never let me down. I had a lot of pent up frustration and anger and I could not wait to release it on our next opponent. All of us wanted to snap out of our five-game losing streak and pay back a team who had defended us the first game of the season: Charlotte.

My frustrations were mended and we handed Charlotte a 68-63 loss. It felt great to get a little payback and it was starting to feel like we were coming along as a team. Rita, who had become one of my closest friends, whispered in my ear as we made our way off the court that Steve had been drafted No.2 to Vancouver. I was excited for him, but felt an odd twinge that he'd be playing so far away. When I got to my room I turned on the television to see where the rest of my friends had been drafted. I was shocked when all the reports were talking about Steve's reaction. He should have been doing back flips, but the look on his face was one of frustration and disappointment. His childhood dream had just come true and here he was on TV looking like a spoiled brat. He told me on the phone that he hoped and prayed that his agents would be able to come to a compromise with the team and be able to work out a trade.

That night Steve called me from his draft party. He told me how he wished I could have been there with him to celebrate. We laughed and joked about all of his new "friends" who were there attending the party. He told me how he didn't know who was real and who was just along for the ride. I encouraged him to enjoy the moment and to figure out the rest later. He laughed and said he would call me tomorrow. And then he told me he loved me.

Rita was jumping around, just waiting for me to get off the phone. As soon as I hung up she blurted out, "Mique, you know Steve likes you!" I said, "No! We are good friends and have a lot of similarities, but that's it." She said, "Well, maybe you think that way, but he likes you." I downplayed the situation, because I didn't feel anything for Steve outside of being a friend. I grew up having more guy friends than girls and felt comfortable having platonic relationships with men. I thought everyone was putting too much energy and effort into something I just didn't feel or see.

When I arrived back to DC that afternoon, Larry and I ate a late lunch in Old Towne Alexandria. As always, I was happy to see him. Over lunch he talked about how he was looking forward to seeing his family in Chicago, especially his son Devin. I never thought I would ever date a man who had children, but he changed the way I viewed men with children. I loved that being a good father was important to him.

But as we were eating lunch that day the tone of the conversation shifted suddenly from carefree and easy to heavy and difficult. He asked me if I was sure I wanted him in DC. I was conflicted: the words out of my mouth said I wanted him there, but inside I wasn't as sure. His constant questioning of me, our bickering and his insecurities were infiltrating our relationship. He was becoming more like a father figure, questioning my every move and decision. The other part of me wanted to work through that. I attributed his concern to him being five years older and a little more mature. However, I wasn't prepared for what he said next. He asked me if I was having an affair with one of my female teammates. I was insulted. His accusatory remarks infuriated me and I immediately told him no. I left the restaurant that day confused and angry.

After dropping another game to Sacramento a few days later, I prepared mentally for Larry to be gone the next week and a half. Our time apart would give me time to think and hopefully erase the tension we'd been having. I hated feeling like I had to walk on eggshells around him. I felt like I had to compromise so much of myself just to keep the peace between us. I had some serious thinking to do concerning my relationship.

A week or so had passed, and Larry and I were starting to communicate better and I was looking forward to him coming home. I seemed like all we needed was some time apart to reflect on some things and really appreciate each other. I was able to clear my head and rationally think about my relationship with him. Things were really looking up for us. However, everything changed when I received a call from him making the same accusations once again. I thought we were beginning to move past all of this, but we were in the same position. After a few childish words were exchanged, my emotions took over me. I yelled to him over the phone, "I can't do this anymore! I'm tired! It's over." I hung up and tears started to pour from my eyes. I shook and cried as I sat in our home, in our bed, numb over what had just happened. I could not believe that those words had just left my mouth.

The next morning, I had to head to the airport for our game against the Detroit Shock. I was in pieces, totally destroyed by what had happened between Larry and me. I walked into the airport and Rita asked me what was wrong. Tears started to flow down my face before I could get any words out. She knew it was something serious and pulled me over to a quiet and less crowded area. I sobbed on her shoulder and she consoled me with a hug. I collected myself just enough to tell her what had happened. Rita advised me to take some time to think about things before I made any final decisions. She said, "If it's worth fighting for, then fight for it." I wiped the tears from my eyes and took what she said into consideration.

Larry called me once we landed in Detroit. I told him I really didn't want to talk and that it would be best for us both to move on. He kept telling me to calm down and that I was overreacting. I'm sure his words were meant to calm me, but somehow they just annoyed me more. One insult led to another and finally our conversation came to a close with me asking him to FedEx me his keys. I was officially done with our relationship.

No matter what was going on off the court, I had a job to do on the court. We were on a two-game win streak, but things quickly went south and the month of July was extremely disappointing for everyone. We were a dismal 4-14 and everyone was frustrated. Nikki McCray and I were putting up good numbers, but who cares about numbers when your team is getting worked every night. I was waiting for Coach Darsch to crack her whip as Coach Summitt would have, but it never happened. Instead we got a watered-down version of discipline. I guess I was expecting one of those Pat Summitt speeches where she just rips into everyone and everything is left out in the open. What I didn't realize was that every coach is different in their approach, and pro basketball is not just about x's and o's but also about managing personalities. Coach was doing her best to make us gel as a team, but nothing seemed to be working.

I was finally beginning to understand the distinct difference between college and the pros. In college, Coach got the best players in the country to commit to play together year in and year out. She got the best players in the country to selflessly give of themselves for the better of the team. She would drill into people and somehow bring the best out of them. She would get us as children and we would leave the university as women.

But pro coaches get us as women and so we're a little more opinionated and outspoken, which comes from living and making decisions. I was physically prepared, but the mental toll was far greater than I was prepared for. Someone like Pat Summitt built Tennessee's program, and she will probably coach there as long as she likes. She does not get pressure from management to make decisions like pro coaches do. There were times I'd make a bad play and expect Coach Darsch to rip me a new one but instead I was met with words of encouragement. I would hear, "You got the next one, Mique!" and I didn't understand why she wasn't all over me. What I did know was that she met with me constantly to discuss basketball and to help me adjust to the pro game. She knew I wasn't used to losing and tried to keep my spirit up. Maybe she didn't yell at me constantly because she knew I had a lot of pressure on my shoulders. At 21, I was fresh out of college, after playing for arguably the best women's basketball coach ever. I was searching for Pat Summitt, but she was long gone.

One week after a tough practice, our assistant coach Melissa McFerrin caught me in the hall as I was leaving the arena. I thought it was going to be the normal chitchat we always exchanged, but today she wanted to talk to me about trust. I remember telling her trust is something that people earn and I just couldn't go around putting my trust in everything and everyone. She said it was about having blind faith and she asked me if I understood what she meant by blind faith. I told her sure, it's believing in something that you may not fully understand. I went on to tell her how my grandmother had blind faith when she took my brother and I in so we didn't have to go to foster care. She didn't know what it would be like to raise two young children in her 50s, but she took a chance anyway.

McFerrin smiled at me and said, "Well then, think about that wall you have up and start letting people in."

I was starting to feel misunderstood. Was my new team taking my quiet disposition the wrong way? I had always been quiet and it took me time to warm up to people. I decided I didn't have to be best friends with everyone. I just needed to do my job to the best of my ability. I learned that I couldn't let things people said affect me so deeply.

I started to pick up the pieces of my life off the court, at least. Things were starting to feel normal again. I decided that it was best that Larry and I keep our distance from each other until we healed from our breakup. To fill the big hole he left in my life, I spent time with friends doing things around the city when I wasn't on the court. Steve and I began to spend time together again. Rumors swirled that we were dating whenever we were seen together. I was constantly telling people that we were just friends, but my defense was usually shot down with an eye-roll.

One rare day off, Steve called and told me he was coming to pick me up to get my mind off ball. We spent the day shopping and he took me to my favorite restaurant, which was Ruth's Chris. He knew exactly how to get my mind off things. When he dropped me off I innocently offered him my spare bedroom. We were both tired from the day's activities and I didn't want him to have to drive home. He declined and looked at me as if I'd asked him to rob a bank with me. I shrugged and said okay and told him to call me when he made it home.

Before I could make it to my bedroom I got a call from him. He confessed that his feelings for me had grown and he no longer wanted to just be my friend. He told me that he was very attracted to me and didn't want to overstep or disrespect me in any way by staying the night. I had no idea that he felt that way. At the end of the conversation he asked me if we could hang out the next day and I agreed.

The next day after practice we hung out and we probably looked like two school kids on the playground just smiling and blushing as if we were just meeting for the first time. At the end of the day when he was dropping me off at home he leaned over and told me he wanted to kiss me. It was an awkward moment and I didn't know what to say. The next thing I knew he put his hands on my face and pulled me toward him. I closed my eyes, held my breath, and the inevitable occurred. After that night, we started dating.

It seemed like it was a fresh start for me both off and on the court. For the first two weeks of August we played some amazing basketball. I don't know what happened, but we finally started clicking. Things were really looking up for the franchise. Steve and I were having fun, and he was so supportive of me. He even managed to pull off a surprise party for me for my birthday. He kept telling me he was busy with meetings and would not be able to take me out to dinner or celebrate my birthday with me. I was disappointed, but understood. Plus he had already given me an amazing early birthday gift. The morning of my birthday I met with Sashia, who had introduced us, for breakfast. She came over to pick me up to take me to my favorite breakfast spot. As she waited for me to finish getting ready, the doorbell rang. I opened my door and there stood a deliveryman holding a huge bouquet of beautiful white roses. Attached was a note from Steve that read, "Good morning! The flowers are for our new beginning. Enjoy your day." It was such a sweet gesture especially since we would not be spending my birthday together. I sent him a message and thanked him for the flowers. I put the flowers in some water and then headed out the door to find a car service waiting for us. I looked at Sashia with a surprised expression and she simply said for me to just go with the flow and not ask any questions. We went to breakfast and then to the spa for some pampering. Once I finished, Sashia said we were going to lunch and the car service took us to the Georgetown Waterfront to Sequoia for some wonderful seafood. When I got to my table there were beautiful yellow roses waiting for me. After we arrived, Steve texted me and asked if I was enjoying myself. He then asked if I knew what yellow roses meant.

Moments later I received another message explaining their meaning. He said that yellow meant friendship, the basis of any good relationship. Just after we ordered our food, I felt a tap on my shoulder. I turned around thinking it was our server, but to my surprise there was Steve standing there. He wrapped his arms around my waist and gave me a big hug. He had a huge smile on his face and told me that he wouldn't miss my birthday. It was the first time anyone had surprised me like this and I felt really special. I figured we were headed back home after lunch, but I was wrong. We headed over to Six Flags to play games and ride roller coasters. Anyone who knows me knows I love amusement parks.

After leaving the amusement park he had the driver drop me off home so I could shower and get ready for dinner. He then went to get his truck and to head home and get dressed too. He picked me up and we headed to our favorite restaurant, Ruth's Chris. At the table waiting were two dozen red roses. During dinner we must have drunk two bottles of wine. Steve kept refusing drinks because he had to drive us home but told me to drink as much as I wanted because it was my day. I was really tipsy as we headed back to my house. When we pulled up to my house, Steve asked me for my keys, walked to my side of the car and opened my door. As I stumbled from the car, I hugged him so tightly. He walked me to the door, slowly turned the key and pushed the door open. As he opened the door I heard the roar of people inside yelling "Surprise!" I stumbled through the door and around the room, thanking everyone for coming. We had cake, chatted and listened to music as the night went on. I could not believe that Steve had done all of this without me knowing.

Soon the summer was coming to an end and my first WNBA season was just about over. Though we would not make the playoffs, we were a much-improved team from the previous year. We went from 3-27 to 12-20 and the future looked promising. I finished the season averaging 16.9 points and won WNBA Rookie of the Year and received Second Team All WNBA Honors. At the season's end I was exhausted. As soon as the season was over I spent time in DC for a week or so before heading down to Houston to visit Steve. When I arrived he showed me around the city and took me to eat. While we ate dinner he showed me pictures of the house he was planning to purchase and I was really excited about seeing it. I stayed for a while but didn't know anyone, so when Steve went out of town for games I would hang out with his brother Terry and Tina Thompson, who played for the Houston Comets. Tina and I had become friends since meeting in Louisiana my senior year when she attended my game.

After a few weeks in Houston, I had to leave to join the national team for USA basketball. It was important for our USA team to train several times throughout the off-season to prepare for the 2000 Olympics. We trained in Colorado Springs and then headed to Europe for exhibition games. My favorite places we played were Italy and Argentina. I loved the historical buildings and museums. I would wander through the cities where we played taking picture after picture. It was such an honor traveling around the world and getting to see such beautiful places.

When I arrived home from my travels with the national team I flew to Los Angeles to shoot my first commercial for Nike. Raye Pond contacted me to talk about the concepts of the commercials. The first idea they had was about dolls and the other would be me reciting Psalm 23. I could not relate to the first concept, because I never really played with dolls, but Psalm 23 rang close to home for me. It was the prayer I had recited over and over and was near and dear to my heart. This commercial would not only be a direct reflection of me, but it would also represent my grandmother. I understood I would be putting myself out there for criticism because of my religious beliefs, but I took the chance. The Lord's Prayer had been my comfort through all of the adversity in my life and I wanted to share it. I had similar feelings when *Slam* magazine put me on the cover my senior year at Tennessee. I wore a NY Knicks jersey and many people didn't know how to interpret it. Some thought it was a statement saying I was good enough to play in the NBA and bordered on arrogance. For me it brought back the memory of the letters I wrote to myself as a kid that saying I was going to be the first girl to play in the NBA. To this day, I'm the only woman to have ever graced the cover of *Slam*.

After the commercial shoot in L.A I returned to New York to spend some much needed down time with my family and friends. With a crazy schedule it was nice to get a little TLC from my grandmother. Though I had traveled around the world and seen some of the world's most beautiful places, my grandmother's apartment in the projects was home to me. While I was there it seemed like the knocks at our door were endless. Everyone wanted to give their congratulatory words. My grandmother was so proud of me and would share my story with anyone who would listen.

One day I took my grandmother to look at nearby condos in Astoria. I wanted to buy her a new place where she could stretch out and be happy. No matter how much I insisted, she told me she was happy where she was. She was happy to have her health, friends, and peace of mind. She said she would come visit me whenever I wanted her to, but that she would not move out of the projects. I finally accepted her decision. Besides, to finally have enough money to take my grandmother and family out to a nice restaurant meant the world to me. I had come so far.

After my week in New York I headed back home to Virginia. I was barely home when I received a call from my mother in a panic. I told her to calm down because I couldn't understand her through her sobbing on the other end. My heart began to race and I instantly thought something had happened to someone in my family. As I was talking to her my grandmother called on the other line. So I asked my mother to hold and I clicked over to my grandmother. My grandmother's voice sounded sad and shaky on the other end and I grew more and more worried. I clicked back over to my mother and told her I would call her back.

I could tell my grandmother had been crying. She finally began to tell me what happened. She proceeded to tell me she had been keeping a secret. Her voice was shaky when she told me that Thurman McGee Holdsclaw was not my grandfather. I quietly listened on the other end. She told me that my mom's father was a man named Sonny Hicks and that my mom was born on Langley Air Force Base near Hampton, Virginia. Sonny drank a lot and when my mother was three he verbally and physically abused my grandmother after one of his drunken stupors. He picked my mother up and held her out the kitchen window, saying he would kill them both if she didn't do as he said. After my grandmother pleaded with him for several minutes he pulled her in and left my mom in the kitchen sink. The next morning, when he left the house for work my grandmother packed up my mom and a few items and with very little money bought a bus ticket to New York. Her sister lived there and she knew that the two of them would be safe with her. After a few years of life in New York she met and eventually married Thurman Holdsclaw. Thurman always treated my mom as his own so my grandmother never said anything. Each year that went by it got easier and easier to forget the truth. The only reason why the truth was ever uncovered was because Sonny's family started seeing my name on television. They started reading articles and soon found out that June was my grandmother and Bonita was my mom. Sonny's sister called my grandmother several times trying to put the puzzle together and my grandmother finally told her it was true. My grandmother finally got enough courage to tell my mother the truth and when she did my mother lost it. I did my best to comfort my grandmother and assured her that we would get through this as we had with everything else.

After I hung up with my grandmother I called my mom back. I could tell she was really upset. I let her know I would be there for her if she needed me. She said she had spoken to her biological father and was going to meet him the following weekend. I told her I would fly up to New York to be with her. Honestly, I could have cared less to meet a man who abused my grandmother and threatened to harm an innocent child. But I knew my mom needed to do this because her identity had been altered so abruptly. I also thought about the fact that I was carrying a name that I had no blood connection to.

That next weekend I flew into LaGuardia, picked my mom up in Staten Island where she resided, and head to visit the Hicks family. Immediately upon entering their residence in New Jersey I saw a man who greatly resembled my mom. They had very similar builds, but nothing stood out more to me than their eyes. They were the same shape and hazel color. They both cried as they hugged each other for the first time. For the first time I could understand where the other side of my mother had come from. Over the next few weeks my grandmother and mom worked out their issues. Sonny Hicks became a part of my mom's life until he passed away three years later to an undisclosed medical condition. Though her time with him was short, I know that she is grateful to have gotten the chance to know him. A lot was happening with my family, but I had a busy life to get back to.

Since I was named a member of our National Team the Olympics were right around the corner. My endorser, Gatorade, contacted me to do a commercial, so I flew back out to LA. The commercial was titled "American Women" and it spotlighted soccer superstar Mia Hamm, track star Marion Jones, and myself. I was so excited because I really looked up to both of them. The commercial featured the song "American Woman," by artist Lenny Kravitz. It was an amazing day in Los Angeles.

While Steve and I were apart we talked all the time. He wanted me there in Houston with him, but understood that I had work to do. He was fine with me being away as long as I was catching his games, especially the highlights. Steve would always know my stats after the game and tell me what I did well with and what I needed to work on. We were competitive with each other when it came to basketball. He would tease me saying that he was going to shoot better from the field than I did, or when he rebounded well he would say that he was looking like me out there. Constantly competing with him helped take the way I trained to another level. Occasionally we would hit the court and he would show me some of his explosive moves.

All of the training I was doing with the USA team and on my own was starting to take a toll on my body. I soon found myself with a stress fracture in my fifth metatarsal. One day as I was cutting at practice I noticed a sharp pains shooting to the side of my foot. I dismissed the feeling at first, but the discomfort grew with each practice. So I told the team. The doctor decided it was best for me to get an MRI to confirm what he suspected. Once the results were in he stressed how important it was for me to rest and let my foot heal. We were at the end of the tour and the last trip was to the 2000 Women's NCAA Tourney for an exhibition game. I still made the trip because I was a part of the team, but I would not be able to play because of my foot. I hated having to sit out. Rita was there supporting UConn, so she was able to come hang out with me and help keep my spirits up. We were both disappointed when we found out the Mystics didn't protect her in the expansion draft, and let the Indiana Fever selected her.

Once our tour was officially over, the doctor told me to stay off my foot for four to six weeks. I was devastated. He explained how if I didn't rest it could require surgery and I could miss the entire season. The doctor's words concerned me and all I could think about was getting to Houston to spend time with Steve. All I wanted was to be comforted. I didn't need a motivational talk everyday, but that's what he gave me. All I heard was "Suck it up, it's going to be okay!" and after awhile it started to sound redundant. I know he was trying to console me the best way he knew how, but it didn't make me feel any better about the situation. We still had our fun being silly and watching basketball highlights and trying new restaurants, but I didn't want to hear his coach-like scolding. I just wanted to enjoy our time together before I had to report back to DC for training camp.

CHAPTER 14

Tipping The Scale

Training camp was now about to start and I was still being held out. It had been about a month since I had done any exercise and I was anxious to get back to doing what I loved. I was eating like I always had, and I started to notice my clothes weren't fitting me the same way. I had a business meeting to go to and my usual custom-made suit didn't fit like it should. I was naïve and figured that my weight gain was muscle, since the trainers had me lifting everyday.

A few weeks into the season I was cleared to hit the court and excited to have WNBA veteran Vicky Bullet join the team. I really respected her as a player and she was a consummate professional that would help bring leadership to our team. I knew she would be a voice in the locker room that people respected. After missing all of our preseason games, I started getting phone calls from close folks asking me if I was pregnant when I first came back to play. I didn't realize that I had gained that much weight. After the game I immediately called Steve to ask him what he thought. He agreed that I had gotten a little thicker, but that he didn't think it was a bad thing. He encouraged me by saying that I would lose the weight as I got back in shape. During the process of playing and losing the weight my feet would ache so bad. The whole season my heels felt like I was walking on rocks and I continually had to sit out of practice. I couldn't lose the weight I needed to because I couldn't practice regularly and my friends and family told me that the fans were starting to talk.

It bothered me, but we had so much other drama going on with the team that my imaginary pregnancy was the least of our problems. One moment it was Vicky and Nikki getting on each other nerves. Next, it was me getting annoyed with the situation as a whole. I felt like we were on an island that was sinking quickly. Over this time Murriel Page and I had started to establish a friendship. She was always positive and worked hard everyday. She did all of the intangible things that makes a person a good teammate. She was slowly becoming the glue that held our team together.

There was all this talk about our team finally having a Big Three. The term meant the team had three reliable players that could produce. We were compared to the Houston Comets. However, they were winning championships and we were barely winning games. The frustration was often palpable. Nikki went into a hole and wouldn't talk to anyone because she felt no one liked her. My game was suffering and for the first time in my career I was substituted from the game in a critical situation. The game was close in the fourth quarter and Coach Darsch substituted me out of the game. The clock ticked down as I sat on the bench, fuming. I thought we could have won had I stayed in the game. I was so furious and made a comment on the bench to my teammates that I thought she quit on us. One of my teammates Markita Aldridge, who was an outspoken player, looked at me and told me calm down. She didn't want to see my actions turn ugly in front of the fans. So I shut my mouth and watched my team take another loss. Back in those days I operated mostly off of emotion and told the media I felt Coach benched me for no reason. The next day the media published my comments and all of what I said was blown out of proportion.

Sashia came to the locker room before practice and said Wes Unseld, our General Manager, sent her over to tell me Michael Jordan wanted to talk to me. Michael Jordan was now the President of Washington Sports, which oversaw the men's and women's teams. I was so nervous and had no idea what he wanted to talk to me about. So I quickly left the locker room and headed to his office. I waited in the lobby before entering his smoke filled office. Cigar smoke filled the air at 9:30 in the morning. I entered the room and he told me to sit down and listen. He told me he had supported me when Nike wanted to sign me, when Gatorade did the commercial with me, and now he was urging me to shut up and never talk about a coach to the media again. He told me to focus on playing and being the best player I could be. He then asked me whom I ultimately thought the fans would keep: the player or the coach? He said, "The player, so just let the fans get rid of the coach." He went on to explain how he had a tough time early in his career with his coach, Doug Collins. I was sent to apologize to Coach Darsch for what I had said to reporters. The situation on our team wasn't because we didn't have good coaches, but it was because there was too much childish drama on our team and a serious lack of communication.

Before practice, my team and I were asked to go back to the locker room for a meeting. We all sat in our lockers and waited for the coaches to come in. Melissa McFerrin, our assistant coach, came in and announced that Coach Darsch had resigned. We were all surprised, but the majority of us felt a change was needed. I wondered if she resigned because of what I had said. I really wanted to apologize. Over the next week people speculated that I had gotten the coach fired, which of course made me angry.

After her resignation, Darrell Walker, a former NBA player, was appointed our interim head coach. He immediately let it be known that we had messed up his summer. He'd been enjoying playing golf and spending time with his family. Therefore, we needed to work hard and compete. He changed things around for what he thought was for the better. We were all optimistic and we hoped that the changes he made would help us win. He was straightforward and held us accountable for our work on the court. If you didn't play hard he sat you down. The team chemistry and overall environment improved and he told us he was going to treat us just like he would treat his male pro players. He told us to focus and come to practice prepared to work hard. He wanted practices to be short and intense. He didn't think it was necessary to be in the gym for two to three hours practicing. He said an hour and a half was enough time to practice if we went hard and got through what we needed to work on. Nowadays, many coaches in the WNBA have adopted that frame of thought, especially since most of the women play year round. We were all tired of losing and we did our best to buy into the new changes.

Around midseason I finally stepped on a scale and it read 185. The season before I played at about 170, but while resting to let my foot heal I had gained 15 pounds. I had never had a problem with my weight and didn't know how to fix it. I didn't have teammates or coaches talk to me about it so I truly didn't know anything was wrong. It was until Coach Summitt flew in to see one of my games that I knew I had a problem. She couldn't believe the weight I had gained. After the game we went out to dinner and she told me I looked a little out of shape. Hearing those words come from her was a serious wake up call. She had always been honest with me and I really respected what she had to say. So I did my best to watch what I ate and I did extra cardio to try and drop a few pounds.

Despite all the issues we had that season, we ended up making it to the playoffs with a 14-18 record. We made it to Eastern Conference Semifinals before losing to the NY Liberty, 2-0. After our loss, Coach Darrell went off on every player on the team. He told each person what she needed to work on in order for us to get to the next level. He told us all the things we needed to do but didn't want to hear. He told some players they needed to stop partying, drinking beer, and get in shape. His list of things we needed to improve on went on and on. When he got to me he told me I wasn't the leader my team needed me to be. He thought I needed to be more like Teresa Weatherspoon. She was cocky and carried herself with a huge amount of confidence. He thought I needed some of that cockiness to lead everyone in this locker room. He said I had the skill and that he listened to me talk nonstop on the bus, so he knew I could do it. He then went on to say that they wanted to follow me, but they needed a reason to. His tone and words pierced us, but we all needed to hear the things he said.

We had made the playoffs for the first time in franchise history and had come a long way. However, many felt like we had underachieved because of all the talent we had on our team. I improved statistically across the board, but I wasn't added to any of the All-WNBA teams. I felt it was because of the way my game had changed due to the weight gain. I was doing a lot more posting up and wasn't moving the same on the court. I also felt that my public criticism of the coach also had factored into how I was perceived. My antics had made a lot of people fall out of love with me.

After the WNBA season was complete, I had a little more than a week to spend with Steve, who had been in DC often that summer, before I had to leave to prepare for the Olympics. Once I met up with the USA team in preparation for the Olympics, things started to really unravel for me. It seemed like my weight gain was the topic of everyone's conversation. When we arrived in Sydney, Australia for the Olympics, my foot started to hurt again; I felt the same sharp pain I had with my previous injury. I got another MRI and it revealed that I had two stress factures in the same right foot. It was my third metatarsal and the cuboid bone. My dream of playing in the Olympics was crushed and I was devastated. When the higher up officials with the team found out about my injury, they asked me if I wanted to go home and I began crying. I had worked just as hard as anyone to get there and I had earned the right to enjoy the experience. I talked to some of the older players about the situation and they urged me to stay. I had worked for this and earned my place on the team. I decided to stay. Besides, my mom, grandmother, and Aunt Pat had all made the trip to support me. So I hobbled around Sydney doing whatever I could to support my team in their quest for gold. We ended up winning the gold and it was amazing feeling. The moment the gold medal was placed around my neck was surreal. I was filled with pride to be a part of the best in the world, even though I hadn't been able to play like I wanted to.

Once I returned from the Olympics I started house hunting. I had gotten the opportunity to know the DC area better and had an idea of where I wanted to live. I decided I want to stay in Alexandria, Virginia and found a subdivision I really liked. I knew living there was meant to be when the home I like the most was located on lot No.23.

After I purchased my new home I called coach Summitt to share my news. During our conversation she told me that I needed to come back to Knoxville to get back in shape. She thought that my weight could be the reason I was getting stress fractures. I thought about it for a good couple of minutes and finally agreed to come once my foot healed. She told me to call Jackie Ansley from Performance Training, which was based in Knoxville. She was confident Jackie could get me back into tiptop shape in no time. Jackie had worked with our team throughout my career in college so I felt comfortable with her. I'm not going to lie; I wasn't excited about going back to Knoxville. I wanted to relax and enjoy my new house. But after our conversation I stepped on the scale in my bathroom and it read 188 and I knew I had to go.

In early November I started the drive from Alexandria to Knoxville. It took almost seven hours to get there. I rented a furnished apartment in a new apartment complex in West Knoxville and for the next three months I worked out four days a week twice a day. During the first month, Jackie almost killed me with cardio workouts and lifting. Our morning sessions usually lasted two hours, then I would go to my apartment eat a good lunch, and nap. The second sessions went from four to six. We started with cardio and then hit the court to do a low impact basketball workout. Our Tuesdays and Thursday mornings consisted of pool workouts and in the evenings, more cardio and weights.

I stuck with it and also started to learn about nutrition. I started eating a lot more fresh vegetables and lean meats. I made smarter choices when eating and dropped McDonalds and other fast food restaurants from my diet. During this time, Steve was very supportive, but our schedules were both hectic and that cut down on the amount of time we spent together. We still spoke throughout the day and before we went to bed, but the distance between us grew.

When December came around it was time to step up my training even more. We were still doing cardio hard before each session, and now Jackie incorporated SAQ (Speed, Agility and Quickness) into my workouts. On-court conditioning and pick-up games also increased in intensity. I was starting to see a change in my body, but it wasn't easy. One morning I had just finished a 45-minute cardio workout on the cross trainer and was about to lift weights when I broke down. Jackie put her hand on my shoulder and let me know it was okay. The stress of everything had taken a toll on me and I didn't know if I was coming or going. To make things worse Steve and I decided to take a break from dating. It was a mutual agreement. There was no bickering or fighting and we both agreed that things were going in another direction. I know I wasn't as attentive as a girlfriend like I had been before I began training.

During that time Steve had become more of a motivational coach than a boyfriend and it bothered me. I had several close male friends who were athletes so I knew all about their lifestyle. He had become the star of the Houston franchise and I'm sure girls were all over him. He would tell me stories of the lengths some women went through to try to get to his attention. I was never jealous and I was always a firm believer that everyone needs to experience life and everything it has to offer. All that I asked was for him to be honest with me about what was going on. I have always appreciated that Steve was a great communicator and was honest with me.

Despite what I was going through personally, I continued to work hard. By the time I had finished working with Jackie I had lost 18 pounds and was in amazing shape. Everyone in my circle was so proud of me, but I was even more proud of myself. When I finished training in February, I headed back home to Virginia. I connected with some guys in the area and started going to a gym called Run and Shoot daily. I would play and do my cardio workouts and weight program Jackie made for me. I was determined to maintain the physical form I had worked so hard to get back. I suffered through my last WNBA season and I did not want to ever have to endure something like that again.

Even though Steve and I had broken up, we still continued to talk every other day or so. After one of our conversations, he invited me to come to Houston to check out a few of his games and spend time with him and his family. His grandmother, Mrs. Wilson, was in town and we connected well because she reminded me so much of my grandmother. Over the course of our dating, Steve's family had become mine and I really enjoyed spending time with them. People didn't understand how we couldn't be together, but still be around one another. After spending time with Steve and his family, I headed back to DC to prepare for the upcoming WNBA season.

CHAPTER 15

Renewed

Before the season began I was called by management and told that Wes Unseld had resigned as our general manager and that Melissa McFerrin would be taking over. Tom Maher was named our new head coach. Tom Maher was the Australian National Team Coach, I didn't know much about him, but I was excited about the addition of Marianne Stanley, his assistant. She had the reputation of being a no-nonsense coach and I though that would be great for our team. I was excited about all of the changes and hoped they would translate to success on the court.

I started that season very optimistic. I continued learning from Vicky Bullet; she always passed on little tidbits to me to help me improve as a professional. She told me how important it was to ice after practice and games. She promised me it would help keep my legs fresh. I appreciated the new energy we got from our new coach, and wanted him to know I was behind him 100%. I tried my hardest to rebuild my image and be supportive. Unfortunately, Tom's debut in America as a WNBA coach didn't go well. His coaching style was very different than what we were used to. Many of the players weren't sold on his philosophy and we looked disjointed out there on the court for most of the season. We had a disappointing season going 10-22 and finished eighth in the Eastern Conference. Following the season Tom resigned as head coach, as did Melissa McFerrin. I had just finished my third year as a pro and had gone through three different coaches. I was looking for consistency of some sort, but there was none. We were a team struggling to find our way without a leader. I knew that management was going to make some changes once again, but they were pretty hush about it.

During the off-season I spent my time working out between DC and Knoxville. I even headed to Orlando a few times to workout with shooting coach Chip England. I felt like I needed to improve my shot. I had watched a game tape of myself and I noticed it didn't look smooth and that my shot was flat. I'd also shot a career low from the field (.400) and from free throw line (.682) that season. If I wasn't working on my game I was in the community working with the Verizon Literacy Program. I was trying my hardest to improve as a player and person.

I was starting to learn to take control of my own life and how to set boundaries for myself and other people. I was coming into my own and becoming a lot more opinionated. This time was really exciting for me. I knew I had responsibilities, but I stopped trying to please everyone. I started to write more and my journals started fill up quicker than they ever had before. My taste in music, clothes and literature even changed. For the first time I didn't care what people thought; I was finally comfortable in my own skin. A quote from Dr. Seuss became my mantra during this time: "Be who you are and say what you feel because those who mind don't matter and those who matter don't mind." I was happy with the person I was evolving into.

It was time for our USA National Team to start preparing for the World Championships, like we had over the previous years. Van Chancellor was named head coach and I was looking forward to it. He was a fun guy and had won several championships as the head coach of the Houston Comets. The team met in Houston to train. I came straight from Knoxville, where I had been training with Jackie for the past month or so. I was looking better on defense, rebounding the ball well, and getting up and down the court like I had when I was in college. Offensively my shot had improved and I was starting to feel like my old self. I competed against Sheryl Swoopes in scrimmages since we played the same position. I was focused on doing little things while creating scoring opportunities for my team by hitting the offensive boards and keeping the ball alive on plays. However, what I was doing wasn't enough. All the other coaches said I looked great, but Van Chancellor thought I was out of shape. I honestly couldn't believe he thought that, especially how I had been playing. I called Jackie, who was one of my toughest critics, and she was shocked by his remarks. It put a sour taste in my mouth, but I didn't let it bother me. I just pushed myself to work harder. I knew how much work I had put in and I knew that I was ready to play.

A few weeks later we headed to the 2002 NCAA Women's Final Four for practices and an exhibition game. I was excited that I was going to get to spend time with my Tennessee family. They had once again made it back to the Final Four. Practices were going well, but Van was constantly in my ear about everything I did. Out of the blue he decided to switch me to the four position and I didn't know the plays. His reasoning behind this was that I could maneuver with limited space and create offensive and rebounding opportunities for the team. I didn't disagree—he was actually right—but he rode me constantly. He would never give me a straight up answer and the feedback I got back from him was always poor. I grew annoyed at the constant nagging. So I did what I'd never done: I decided to leave the team. I ended up meeting with Ann Donovan, our assistant at the time. I told her I was burned out and needed a break. I was off to DC that same day.

I knew some people would be disappointed with me for leaving the national team, but at that time I didn't care. I remember lying in my bed and trying to be silent. I wanted to meditate but I couldn't get my mind clear enough. I kept hearing the phrase, "a new beginning" running through my head. So I looked at my Bible, which was on my dresser, and I opened it. I decided at that moment I was going to change my basketball number. I flipped through the pages and said whatever page I open it to I'm going to change to that number. As soon as I opened it I saw

Deuteronomy 1. I started reading lines 9-13 and what I read mirrored my emotions and what I felt at that point in my life:

> At that time I said to you, "You are too heavy a burden for me to carry alone. The Lord your God has increased your numbers so that today you are as numerous as the stars in the sky. May the Lord, the God of your ancestors, increase you a thousand times and bless you as he has promised! But how can I bear your problems and your burdens and your disputes all by myself? Choose some wise, understanding and respected men from each of your tribes, and I will set them over you.

This seemed to apply to my career because I felt I couldn't carry the burden alone anymore. I needed to let my teammates know how much I needed them and encourage them to have more responsibility. I needed to allow them to do their job and if I was able to do that, we would be more successful as a team. Once I read it, I changed my number to 1.

Our front office decided to make some big changes and shocked everyone by trading Nikki McCray to the Indiana Fever for a player and a couple of draft picks. They also hired Coach Summitt as a consultant and awarded Marianne Stanley the head coaching position. On top of all of that we had two-first round draft picks, the third and fourth to be exact. On draft day we selected Stacey Dales-Schuman, a combo guard from the University of Oklahoma, and Asjha Jones, a versatile forward from the University of Connecticut. They were both talented players and I looked forward to seeing how they would help our team. There was so much newness around me that I couldn't help but feel like it was a fresh start.

I remember when Murriel Page use to joke with me my second year in the league and call me Sybil, saying I had multiple personalities. She said, "Mique, sometimes you are so outgoing, but there are other times when you go into your shell and are so quiet." But the work I had done on myself changed that. One day she pulled me to the side and told me that I seemed so different, but in a good way. She could see that I was a happier person. I went on to tell Page that I had figured some things out and that I had started to love myself.

I wasn't the only one who had changed that season. The Mystics looked like contenders for the first time in franchise history. We owed most of that to Coach Stanley, the best professional coach I have ever played for. She showed the ability to relate to her players and got in our faces when we screwed up. At first I wasn't too thrilled about moving to the 4 position, but she sat me down and explained to me how it would benefit our team. She told me to stop thinking of my role by positions and that the 4 was only defined by a number, not my ability on the floor.

CHAPTER 16

The Last Goodbye

In our first preseason game we looked amazing and everyone was excited about our potential. My grandmother and mother, who had taken the train up from New York to support us, even commented on how good we looked. I was happy to have them both there to see us begin to turn things around. As I was heading back to the locker room I hugged them both and thanked them for coming. I then asked a media person to bring them back to the family room to wait for me. After I finished my interviews a manager came to the locker room to tell me my grandmother was ready to leave and was going to catch the train back home. I exited the locker room to plead with her to stay and she agreed. However, when I finished with my shower and getting dressed she was gone. For whatever reason she decided to take the train home anyway and I was upset.

Later that night she called me and I told her I was upset that she left without waiting or saying goodbye. I thought it was odd because she always stayed and spent time with me. She told me not to be mad and explained why she left. My mother had always been very jealous of the relationship I had with my grandmother and because it was Mother's Day, she didn't want to take away from her time with me. My grandmother thought we needed to spend more time together. She then told me that there would be a day where she would no longer be there and that my mom and I had to work on our relationship. I agreed with her, but I was still mad. I looked forward to spending whatever time I could with my grandmother and I was disappointed that our time had been so short that day. She knew I was still upset and encouraged me not to be. She made a joke and told me she loved me. She said she would be back in a few weeks to cook for me and spend some time. I happily said okay, told her that I loved her, and hung up the phone.

We were looking forward to getting back on our practice court at the MCI Center. They decided to redo the floor, so our preseason practices were held at Marymount University in Arlington, Va. After a tough practice at MU I showered as always and prepared to leave campus. As I walked out of the sports complex I looked at my phone and saw I had several missed calls and messages from my family. I called my Aunt Anita and she told me to come home to New York right away because my grandmother wasn't feeling well. My heart dropped. I told her that I would be home as soon as I could. When I hung up with her I noticed that Donavan, a good friend of my grandmother, had also called so I called him back. He told me she was in the hospital and to please get to New York as soon as possible. He pleaded with me not to drive, but to fly. Panic ran through my body as it never had before. I could feel that something was not right.

I gained enough composure to call my agent who booked my flight to New York while I went home to get clothes. When I finally arrived at the airport after the longest drive ever, I parked my car and made my way to the terminal. I stepped up to the ticket counter to get my ticket and I didn't even notice I had begun crying. I could barely get the words out of my mouth but I told the man at the counter that it was a family emergency and that I needed to get home. He printed my ticket and I made my way through the airport to finally board the 40-minute flight home. I sat in my window seat and prayed as I looked out the window. Seconds later the captain came on the intercom and said that the flight would be delayed because something was wrong with the plane. I froze. If there was ever a time I needed to be home quickly, this was it, and here I was stuck on the runway in a plane that didn't work. I sat on that plane for two hours before it was deemed safe for us to fly. During that time, the unmistakable feeling of dread came over my body and sent chills up my spine. Somehow I knew that my rock, my heart, and the one person that had always been there for me was dead. I prayed I was wrong. When my plane landed, my cousin Eric was there to pick me up. He tried to distract me with talk of basketball, but my answers were cold and short. The last thing I wanted to do was talk about basketball. All I wanted was to get home to my grandmother.

When I entered my grandmother's apartment I was instantly reminded of the day I found out my Uncle Thurman had passed. All of the family was there and when I entered everyone looked up at me and then quickly turned away. No one wanted to tell me the bad news. As I walked by the kitchen to my mother she told me to come into my grandmother's room and sit down. She put her hand on my leg and looked me in my eyes and said two words: "She's gone." I screamed and cried. I hadn't even gotten a chance to say goodbye. The moment I heard those two words leave my mother's mouth, a piece of me died too.

After about five minutes, I wiped my face and began going about the business of masking my feelings. Someone needed to be strong for the family and I decided it had to be me. I knew everyone would look to me for direction during this time. So I did my best to pull myself together. My mother informed me that my grandmother had passed away some time between 8:00 and 10:00am. My Aunt Hattie, my grandmother's sister had talked to her around eight when they made plans to meet at ten in the back of her building so they could go their nails done. My aunt Hattie arrived as planned and waited for my grandmother. After waiting five minutes she called my grandmother's house, but got no answer. Finally, after several attempts to contact her, my brother picked up the phone. He had been at my grandmother's house spending the night. He went into her room to tell her that the phone was for her. He shook my grandmother to wake her up but she didn't move. He tried again and again before he noticed that she wasn't breathing.

As I heard the story all I could think of was how my grandmother told me that my mother and I had to work on our relationship because she wouldn't always be here. It was as if she knew her time here was almost up. My heart was broken, but I had to be strong for my family, especially for my mother and my brother. I feared my grandmother's death would drive my mother back to drinking and that the ten years of sobriety would be flushed down the drain. My grandmother had been the glue of my family and now everything threatened to come apart at the seams. I stayed home with my family and helped with the arrangements for her wake and funeral. The regular season was about to start, but I had to take care of my family first. As I made arrangements I asked Coach Summitt to share a few words at her funeral. My grandmother had loved her and I knew she was grateful for the role Coach Summitt had played in my life.

On the day of the funeral I was numb. Her service was beautiful and everyone had amazing things to say about my grandmother. When it was time for Coach Summitt to speak she shared some stories about my grandmother that made everyone laugh. She talked about her getting into the Final Four without a ticket and how she had been escorted by security to the Tennessee area without anyone ever asking her who she was. She talked about her spirit and how people gravitated toward her. After Coach Summitt's words I delivered the eulogy. I stood among my family and friends to talk about the woman who had raised me. It wasn't until I looked ahead and saw Steve crying that I got choked up. It was a hard day, but I did my best to put on a brave face. The most difficult part of my day was going to the burial site and watching them put her in the ground. It hurt me to the core, but no tears left my eyes.

Just as I did as a child, I used basketball as my medicine to cope. I put all my feelings and energy into basketball and I had one of my best seasons as a pro leading the league in scoring and rebounding. I averaged 19.9 ppg and 11.6 rpg—essentially, I played out of my mind. I was the front-runner for MVP, but when I went down with injuries to my ankles my chances were crushed. My injuries caused me to miss 12 games and the award was given to someone else. We made amazing strides as a team that season, though, and posted the best record in franchise history 17-15. We finished third in the Eastern Conference finally living up to our talent. We lost in the Eastern Conference Finals to the NY Liberty, but we were back on track.

CHAPTER 17

The Shadow before the Storm

I was still running from my pain when I agreed on a contract to go play in Korea. It was a chance to escape. Months had gone by without a dream of my grandmother but our last encounter constantly ran through my head. All I could think of was her standing outside the locker room in DC and the phone conversation we had that day. I carried around the emotions of that day with me everywhere. I was a ticking time bomb and I feared the moment when all of my emotion would surface, and what shape that outburst might take.

I signed to play for Kookmin Bank in Cheonan, South Korea. It was about an hour train ride to Seoul. I played with my old UT alum Michelle Snow, but I felt so alone. It felt like I was living the same day over and over. I would wake up, go to practice, eat, and then head back to my room to prepare to do it all over again the next day. I would call home to talk to family or listen to music in my free time. There wasn't much for me to do in the city where I played, and the walls began to close in on me. Occasional trips to Seoul for games helped; there I was able to connect with Americans who were stationed on a military base, along with American basketball players on other teams.

My mom and I started talking more and more I tried my hardest to open up and let her in. She was hurting too and I did my best to be there for her. I didn't want her to worry about me. I did my best to pretend that everything was okay. I suffered silently through my time in Korea and when I arrived back in the states, I went to spend time with mom and my dad. I needed to be around my family to try and help heal myself. When I arrived home my dad was once again getting help for his drinking. While in rehab, he was diagnosed with schizophrenia. It was devastating, but I also felt a sense of relief. I finally had an explanation for my father's behavior. The alcohol mixed with his disorder turned him into a person we did not recognize. Once the medication saturated his system, my father became much more alert and stopped talking to himself. He was living in a halfway house in Crown Heights in Brooklyn. He was so happy to see me when I went up to his room. He showed me all the articles he had collected about me over the years. He wanted to know how my body felt and all about my time out of the country. We had a warm, loving visit and for the first time since my grandmother's death I felt happy.

While I was there visiting with my father, my brother stopped by to check on him. My brother and I were not getting along at the time. He had done nothing in school to prepare himself for the future and it frustrated me. I wanted to see my brother out of the projects finding his way as I did, but he had done just the opposite. To help him I had him come to DC the summer before. I got him an apartment and connected him with a tutoring program that would help him get his GED. He didn't have to worry about anything, just wake up and go to class. I knew how difficult the world could be without an education and I didn't want that for him. He took advantage of the situation and used my kindness to fund his summer in DC. One day, I ran into him hanging out in the street when he was supposed to be in class. From that moment on I refused to help someone that wouldn't help himself. My brother and I had always been tight so his poor decisions hurt me. I knew he had a learning disability and I understood his situation, but he had no direction or realistic view of the future. Once, just to see where his head was at, I asked him if he'd rather have a house that was paid off, or a car and some jewelry. He said he would take the car and jewelry.

After some time in New York with my family I returned back home. It felt good to be back in the DMV. I was thankful that the season in Korea was short and allowed me some free time before the WNBA season started again. I stayed in shape by working out with my friend Keith Veney, and I also organized pickup games at the MCI Center when the men didn't have practice. The physical exertion was a great way to keep my mind off the pain I still felt. I had Chip England come up to DC to help me fine-tune some things with my shooting technique. I went from 40% FG/68% FT shooting to 45% FG/83% FT respectively. As long as I had a goal in front of me to work toward, my thoughts we quieted and I didn't feel as much pain. So with the season approaching I put all of my effort and energy into basketball.

Our chemistry in the locker room was great, but unfortunately it didn't translate to the floor. We didn't start the season with the same success as the previous one. At one point we had lost 11 games straight. It was back to the disappointment and frustrated finger pointing. Management came to me to talk about our coach. Other players had complained about her and they wanted to know if I thought she was the reason behind our poor performance. I told them that I felt she had nothing to do with how poor we were playing and that we just weren't coming together or handling business on the court. There was no one to blame but us.

Midway through the season I received word that my grandfather, Thurman Holdsclaw, had passed and that I need to come home for the funeral. He and my grandmother had divorced when their son Thurman Jr. was 12 and had been in and out of our lives since then. He died after a long battle with prostate cancer and I wanted to pay my respects. I didn't know him well, but I wanted to be there for my family. So I purchased my ticket to NY and went up the day before the service. On the day of the funeral I sat in my hotel room on the edge of the bed, thinking of the arguments he had with my mother in the months before he died. He told my mom that I needed to change my last name because it wasn't mine. I had no blood relation to him and he didn't want me to carry his last name. I could not believe that this was the same man who used to pick me up in high school to spend time with me. He would take me to dinner and other places in the city because he wanted to have a relationship with me. Now here he was on the eve of his death, denying me as his grandchild. I couldn't bring myself to leave my room to attend his funeral. Perhaps I didn't go because I wanted to remember him as the kind man who used to spend time with me in high school. I didn't want to remember him as the man who died not wanting me to bear his name. So I just sat in my room the whole day and headed home to DC on the latest flight.

The ups and downs continued that season. We didn't make the playoffs. On top of everything else I sprained my MCL the last game of the season, which added injury to insult. Through it all I prayed that management would keep Coach Stanley. Though we had not had any success that year, I thought it was critical that we keep her on as head coach and continue to build. I had played for the franchise for five seasons and had been through four coaches. All I wanted was consistency. I rehabbed my knee, got healthy, and headed to Valencia, Spain to play for the club there with my teammate, Murriel Page. I really didn't know what to expect and was in a weird space, so I asked my college roommate Zakiah to come with me. She agreed to come if I could cover her bills in the states while she was there. We had so much fun that season and I played really well. Valencia had a good social scene and Murriel, who was fluent in Spanish, showed us around. Zakiah even rented a dance studio and taught hip-hop dance to the locals. We made friends and it really felt like home. Without her there I would have found myself in the same dark place I had been in while in Korea.

But while I was in Spain I received a call from the Mystics' front office saying that Coach Stanley was going to resign and that the organization would be looking for a new coach. I was annoyed that I would be playing for my fifth coach in six seasons.

CHAPTER 18

Things Fall Apart

The organization decided to hire former Washington Bullets player Michael Adams. I was optimistic because I remembered watching him as a kid. He was one of the smallest guys on the court when he played, but he had heart and used to make it rain from the deep with his unorthodox shooting technique. The level of professionalism he brought into our locker room was great. He changed our practices and play schemes into more of a pro style. We had the second pick in the WNBA draft and selected Duke All-American Alana Beard. She was a great combo guard that could help add athleticism on the perimeter and be the solid defensive presence we needed. When we started, all seemed to be going well. We all adjusted to the new coach, his system, and seemed to be making positive progress.

Things were coming together on the basketball side, but on the personal side things weren't as bright. I was having some up and down days, and I started to feel alone even though I had the support of so many people around me. I had no energy to do the things that once made me happy. All I wanted to do was go home to be alone and sleep. I knew something wasn't right, but I was afraid to talk to anyone about it. The sorrow I felt got worse and worse. I would wake up in cold sweats crying and not know why. I was so deep in a hole I was starting to scare myself. Communication with my family and close friends stopped I started drinking to help me cope. A beer or two or a cocktail would help keep the edge off and help me sleep. I had to talk myself into getting out of bed each morning and as I headed to practice I would try to convince myself that I was happy that my sadness wasn't obvious to anyone. I was able to keep this act up for a while before I started to become paranoid. I began to think that everyone was watching me. I felt like my every move was being calculated and criticized, which was true, at least while on the court. It caused me to withdraw from others, and I often found myself sitting at home in the dark, alone.

I sat on the couch in the darkness for days eating Fruity Pebbles between my fits of tears. None of my responsibilities mattered to me and I was completely consumed by the darkness. After a few days of not leaving my house, I saw a note under my door from the doorman. He wanted to make sure I was okay. I had no idea that so much time had passed. After I read his note I was prompted me to check my cell phone. I had several missed called from teammates, agents, and other concerned friends. Somehow, three whole days had disappeared. I called my agent and told him that I was a wreck and that I didn't know if I was going or coming. He told me he would talk to the team and see how they wanted to proceed. The media was aware of my absence and wanted to know what was going on. I realized that I needed help.

Shortly after I decided I needed help, a friend who was a physician knocked at my door. I couldn't figure out how she had gotten to my door because the doorman didn't allow people to enter without the tenant's approval. When I let her in she looked at me in shock. She could barely recognize the person in front of her. She went into my room and got on the phone. When she came back she told me she had called a colleague and gotten the names of a psychiatrist who could see me in the next hour. I pleaded with her that I would be fine and that I just needed a few more days to myself. She yelled at me and told me to take a look around. She opened up the blinds, let sunlight in and told me that I had to go and talk to someone.

I went to that session that day and spent close to three hours with the psychiatrist. She told me what I already suspected: that I wasn't stable, and that my thoughts were irrational. She prescribed me lithium and suggested that I start taking it right away. After our session I went to the pharmacy, filled the prescription and went home. I took the first dosage and immediately started to feel like a zombie. I didn't know any better and thought that this was perhaps an adjustment period. I'd always had a passion for life and now there was a serious disconnect. However, the drug mellowed out my irrational thoughts and made it easier to communicate. I finally was able to have a conversation with my agent and he said the team needed to know what was going on and couldn't understand how their franchise player had all but disappeared. I gave him permission to tell them about my breakdown and that I was now going to a doctor. Thankfully, they were understanding of the situation and supported me. They said that I could take the time I needed.

I spent the next week meeting with the same doctor two hours a day. She told me I had a breakdown as a result of delayed grieving and I laughed. My grandmother had passed away two years ago, and as much as I missed her I know life goes on. She went through all the behavior I had gone through over the years and identified the extreme highs and lows. When I was high I was shopping, fun, and social, and when I was low I was isolated and mean. I sat there in silence. Someone had finally uncovered my secrets and I was able to put words to the thoughts and emotions I mistakenly thought I alone had felt. Over the course of that week it was determined that I was clinically depressed. As we talked, I discovered that I had been dealing with this condition for the greater part of my life. The breakup of my household and my mother's alcoholism marked the beginning of my struggle. For as long as I can remember basketball had been my drug of choice. I would obsessively pour all of who I was into being great and I had finally maxed out on the dosage.

The lithium helped me cope but it really took a lot of energy out of me. I knew being on this medication would make it difficult to return to the sport I loved. In an effort to find some direction I talked to Coach Summitt. Her words for me were encouraging. She told me I could get through this and that I was stronger than I knew. She urged me to fight and get back out there. I've always stood up to her challenges and called my team after speaking with her. I told them I wanted to come back and play. Coach Summitt flew in to support me and gave me a book that helped, *Unquiet Mind: A Memoir of Moods and Madness* by Dr. Kay Redfield Jamison.

I was ready for the challenge, or so I thought. I had to first address my teammates and bring them out of the dark. I apologized for my abrupt departure and told them I had to deal with some personal stuff. I knew my explanation didn't satisfy many of them and playing was like being stuck in a foggy dream. After a game against Detroit, my agent contacted the team and told them that I had decided that it would be best for me to sit out the rest of the season and continue with my treatment. The Mystics supported my decision and I took the rest of the season to heal. The media curiosity over my departure never died down and speculation only increased. People wrote that I was pregnant, had cancer, and one publication even said I had Lou Gehrig's disease. At the time I didn't understand why they wouldn't leave me alone to work out my issues in peace. I later understood that when you don't come out and tell people what is going on, you give them the power to create their own stories.

At this time I was so embarrassed. I didn't want people to know I suffered from depression. I was supposed to be this strong athlete and I didn't want to seem weak in anyone's eyes. So when the team issued a press release saying I was dealing with personal issues, I was fine with that. I remember walking down the street shortly afterwards and having a guy stop me to say I looked fine. He told me that I needed to get back out there on the court and that my team needed me. I was frustrated that most people believed that I had quit on my team. This reminded me that my struggle was internal and people only saw what I looked like on the outside.

CHAPTER 19

The Grass Isn't Always Greener

I continued going to therapy and began to feel like the ground under my feet was solid again, so I made the decision to head back over to Spain for a half season. I decided to stop taking my medication and work through my issues without it. I knew I couldn't perform to the best of my ability while on it and I was anxious to get back on the court. I was doing well and felt in more control than ever. Somehow, I really flourished during my time there, and I was happy.

I decided that I didn't want to play in DC anymore. My mind was clear when I made the decision not to return to the Mystics. So I told my agent that I wanted to be traded. They were against trading me, but I felt strongly about it. I needed a fresh start. To be honest, I was still embarrassed. I didn't feel like I could walk down the street there without someone judging me. All I wanted was a fresh start and in typical Chamique fashion, I dodged my problems instead of facing them headed on.

I really didn't know what I wanted, but when it was announced that I would be traded to the L.A. Sparks, my decision became real. I remember the general manager calling me to welcome me. I thanked her but told her that I wasn't sure if I want to play in the WNBA anymore. She told me to take some time and think about it. She thought I would be a good fit. Eventually the fear of letting people down outweighed my own fears and I agreed to report to camp.

There was a lot of excitement in L.A. about the trade and I soon fell in love with my new surroundings. The team lived three blocks from the beach and the scenery was breathtaking. I convinced myself that I was doing what I really wanted. I did my best to ignore the voice inside of me that knew my heart wasn't into it. I couldn't understand why this beautiful place wasn't for me. The morning of my first meeting with the general manager I decided that I was going to tell her that I had made a mistake. I walked into her office and told her that I didn't want to play. During our meeting she suggested that I connect with a great therapist she'd found to help me with my adjustment. At the end of our meeting I agreed to give it a try. I returned to my apartment and called the therapist. I could now recognize when I was starting to feel overwhelmed and I didn't want things to get out of control again.

The next morning I met with her and we discussed a mapped out a plan of treatment for me. She helped me get on an antidepressant that didn't make me drowsy. I saw her two or three times a week when possible, and she really helped me to adjust. The drugs mixed with the excitement of a new experience covered up the fact I was still being a people pleaser and not truly fulfilling myself. So as I had done in the past, I quieted the inner thoughts and played anyway. My first season in L.A. went on like the other seasons had previously. It was filled with ups and downs and, victories and losses.

Following the season I stayed in L.A. for a few weeks to take in the city and spend time with my friends. I was feeling so great that I stopped taking my medication. I decided that because of my great experiences in Spain that I would sign back to play in Valencia again. I felt that I was functioning well on my own without my medication, and had finally shaken that monkey on my back.

All of that changed when I got word from my mother that my step-father, Freddy, had a cancer that was aggressively invading his body. My heart sank. I offered her words of encouragement and told her I had faith that he would beat this and recover. I told her to pray. I feared what another tragedy would do to me. I tried to stay positive and really believe in the words I had just shared with my mother. I had no control in this situation and all I could do was sit back and pray for the best.

Once the season was over in Spain, I flew back to L.A. The season was already underway with the start of training camp. I loved playing in Spain, but there was nothing like being home. We had a new head coach, Joe Bryant, the father of NBA superstar Kobe Bryant. He had been our assistant the season before and filled in as interim head coach when Coach Bibby resigned. Joe Bryant was a player's coach. He kept the environment stress-free and professional, and I loved his energy. He had great communication skills so when he came to me with an idea I was open and receptive to what he had to say. He told me he wanted to bring me off the bench. He explained how it wouldn't affect my game, but would ultimately help the team. His idea worked and at the end of June we had posted a 12-4 record. We were clicking on all cylinders and having fun. However, the high of success didn't last long for me.

Right before the All-Star break I got a call from my mom saying my stepdad's cancer had advanced. My heart hurt deeply for her. Then, the day after my mom's news, I got a call from my dad's family in South Carolina. They wanted to let me know that my father was doing poorly because he had stopped taking his medication and now he was back wandering the streets and talking to himself. I was angry with my dad's family because I had offered to come down and take him to a clinic and they had declined. He kept telling them he didn't like the way the medicine made him feel so they stopped giving it to him. I felt that they prepared his meals daily and if he was refusing to take it himself, they should have put it in his food. I knew that I had to go see my family as soon as possible.

I was named to the All-Star team that year and had to get permission from the league before I could miss the game. So my team communicated with the league and they allowed me to miss All-Stars. Over the next few days I went to visit my stepfather and father. They only lived three hours from each other, so it was easy for me to drive back and forth. I decided to fly in North Carolina to see my stepdad first. His condition was dire and I wanted to be there for my mother. I wasn't sure what I was thinking, but I definitely was not prepared to see my stepfather like this. Freddie had esophageal cancer and because of his condition he couldn't hold down any food. He was just a frame of skin and bones. He refused to get chemotherapy and was determined to heal his body the natural way. I sat there and held my mother's hand as I watched my stepfather struggle to breathe. I comforted her the best way I knew how, but it was extremely difficult for me to see him like this. Before I left to see my father in South Carolina, I prayed for a miracle. I didn't want to see my mother become a widow or lose my stepfather. I wish I could have spent more time with him, but I needed to make sure my father was okay.

As I drove down to South Carolina my mind was consumed with fear. I had not expected my stepfather to be in that condition and worried what I might find when I got to my father. When I finally found him, it was clear that my dad was mentally gone. He repeatedly asked how my grandmother was doing even though it had been four years since her passing. He had been at her funeral but could not remember that it had happened. He hadn't shaved in weeks and he somehow thought he was Isaac Hayes. I could tell that he had not showered recently and his clothes were soiled with dirt; he looked, smelled and sounded like a homeless person. All of the progress he had made in controlling his mental illness was out of the window. I had no idea how I was going to help him recover from this. I took him to buy new undergarments and clothes. I had to beg him to get a haircut and to take care of himself. I was the only one he would listen to and I prayed that my words would stick because I had to head back to L.A. for work.

When I got back to L.A. I was once again an emotional wreck. I had stopped taking my medication months before and I was flooded with dread. I was so scared to feel what I had felt before so I opened the bottle of meds I had in my apartment and took a pill to calm down. But it was too late and my thoughts we already out of control. My tears turned into rage. I kept mumbling to myself that I was tired as I paced around my apartment. My hands trembled as I called my closes friend in L.A to tell her I was sorry and that I didn't know why this was happening to me. She sat on that phone and tried her best to calm me down. As she was talking to me I took more and more pills. I told her I was tired and that I wanted to sleep and hung up the phone. Minutes after we got off the phone, she was at my apartment knocking at my door. She got me out of my apartment and drove me to an urgent care center. After that moment, things got fuzzy.

When we arrived at urgent care, the doctor on call proceeded to ask me a series of questions. At that point I was drifting in and out of consciousness. My friend told him what I had taken and showed him the bottle. The doctor looked at me and said that he might have to pump my stomach. The next thing I remember was being rushed to nearby Centinela Hospital—they couldn't treat me properly at the urgent care center, apparently.

During my long recovery, I was flooded with shame. I didn't want anyone to know what I had done and was nervous about having visitors to the hospital. To the outside world I had the perfect life. I was successful and doing what I loved. I felt like no one would ever understand why I did this to myself. So after my release from the hospital I met with the owner of our team, Johnny Buss. He wanted to know if I was in or out. I didn't want my secret to get out and being such a people pleaser, I agreed to play. I returned to the team like I wasn't even gone. The team thought I was away dealing with my family. Aside from Murriel, who had come to see me in the hospital, no one had any inclination of what I had been through over the last few days.

The season went on and we made the playoffs. Basketball was once again my medicine and I carried on like I always had. During the playoffs I had a season ending injury in the third game of the first round versus the

Seattle Storm. I tore my plantar fascia on a drive to the basket and had to be carried off the court. I tried to come back and play in the West Conference Finals against Sacramento, but the pain was too much. We finished the season 25-9, improved greatly from the previous season's 17-17.

My suicide attempt changed me. I felt selfish and ashamed. I knew I had great friends and a solid support system and that it was time for me to stop trying to fight my battle alone. I started talking about my attempt to the people close to me and I focused on healing from within. I started to identify which triggers and major occurrences that brought about irrational behavior. I was committed to learning more about my illness. I went back to DC and started regular sessions with my psychiatrist there. Then, just before Thanksgiving, I had surgery on my foot. Once I healed mentally and physically, I headed to Poland to play for Wisla Can-Pack for the second half of the season. I was consistent and on top of taking my pills every day. While in Poland, I got word that the Sparks had fired Coach Bryant and hired Michael Cooper, who had led them to several championships during the franchise's glory years. I was really looking forward to playing for Coop, but I knew I needed to stay focused on my Polish season. We ended up winning the Polish League Championship and it felt good to be apart of a winning tradition again. Basketball was going well and I felt in control of my mental illness. I headed back to L.A. excited about the future and the possibilities.

I know many will ask if I was so truly excited, then why did I leave in this midst of the 2007 season? The reason wasn't because the Sparks had me playing point guard or that I was playing out of position. I understood what I had to do. Tameka Johnson was out with knee problems and I was honestly the only one who could handle the ball and the pressure. Coop used to tell me, "Mique, you got to be a big guard like Magic Johnson and see and distribute the ball, but you have to be smooth and take over the game like Michael Jordan, and have the cockiness and demand the ball like Kobe." Those were high expectations, but they didn't bother me. I did the best I could. Physically, though, the tendonitis in my knees was getting the best of me. I was constantly in treatment and icing. The same week I received an offer from a club in Poland and I took it as a sign. At that point, the pain and the rumors and the back and forth became too much and I had to step away. For the first time I loved Chamique more than any basketball game I would ever play. So with the world watching, for the first time in my life I stepped out of the role of people-pleaser and did something for myself.

CHAPTER 20

Seeking Peace

Walking away that last time was one of the hardest things I have ever done. I knew the effect it would have on my reputation and my legacy, but at the time I didn't care. It was easier for me to be away in Poland and play because no one knew me there and I felt no pressure. When I would play against other teams that had an American on the team, they would ask me why I left the WNBA. I would answer vaguely, saying that I had a lot going on with my family and that I needed to step away.

While I was dealing with my issues, my stepfather was still fighting his battle with cancer. He went to go live at a center for cancer patients where they taught him how to eat healthier and to take care of his body. My mom was extremely upset he would not take chemo, but she supported her husband. He went away for two weeks and I think aside from learning to live healthy he was able to be around other people going through the same thing. A few weeks after he returned home his cell count dropped lower; the cancer did not respond to any of the changes he had made in his lifestyle. So he finally agreed to do chemo. I think that trip emphasized his shrinking options. Chemotherapy wasn't easy, but he fought through it. Our family's prayers were answered, and my stepfather went from being terminally ill to being cancer-free. Four years later, he still is.

The people around me were healing and getting better and it encouraged me to do the same. I realized I had to start talking about what I had gone through. I needed to get rid of the shame that I felt and the only way I could do this was to talk about what I had done. So while I was in Poland I decided to share some of my story with my teammates. I found solace in talking to my teammate Dominique Canty in particular. Dominique and I had been friends since high school. We both came out in 1995, and played in the S.E.C conference against each other. She played her college career at the University of Alabama before playing in the WNBA. Over the course of our time overseas together our friendship grew. For the first time I looked someone in the eye and confessed that I'd tried to commit suicide. She looked at me with a new sense of understanding and finally understood why I had left the league.

It was a small step, but it felt like a weight had been lifted off of my shoulders when I told her. Mentally I was taking steps towards healing, but my knees were still giving me problems. I remember the trainer in Poland telling me about a procedure for tendonitis called P.R.P (Platelet Rich Plasma) Therapy. It is a highly effective non-invasive way to treat the aches and pains I was feeling. They took a blood sample and placed it into a centrifuge. The centrifuge spins and separates the platelets form the rest of the blood components. The entire process takes less than 15 minutes and increases the concentration of platelets and growth factors up to 600%. Using the patient's own blood, specially prepared platelets are then taken and reinjected into the affected area.

It sounded amazing, but there were only a handful of doctors doing this procedure and it wasn't covered by insurance because it was considered experimental. I roughed it out until the Christmas break and settled for a series of cortisone shots. The shots got me through the end of the season. Dominique and I went on to play some great basketball. We helped our team get to the finals before losing in the championship game to our former team, Wisla Can-Pack, 4-3. It was a tough loss, but we all had come a long way and were proud of ourselves.

I came back to the States and received the P.R.P Therapy at Steadman Hawkins Clinic in Vail, Colorado. It was a painful procedure, but three weeks after my treatment all that pain I had experienced in the last year was gone. I felt like a kid again when I played.

When I arrived back in Atlanta, where I was living, I planned my summer. I knew I wanted to travel, so I thought of places I hadn't been and decided I would go. Before any of that I met with a psychiatrist to make sure I was in a good enough place for such activity. This was the first summer I had completely free since before high school. I could do whatever I wanted without having a team to answer to. I could wake up and go to bed whenever I wanted. I could take walks in the middle of the day or take a weekend trip out of town without feeling guilty about any of it. I loved working out on my time and on my terms. I would get in the gym when I felt like it, not when I was told to or out of obligation. I loved and cherished each day and was sincerely grateful that I had been given a second chance at life. That summer I threw my thirtieth birthday party at a swanky club in New York City. I really celebrated that birthday, and was grateful for all the people who showed up. I was high on life and coming into my own.

During that summer, I received a call from my agent telling me that a journalist had contacted him about possibly sharing my story in a public service piece she was doing. When I first heard about the project I wanted nothing to do with it. I wasn't sure that I was ready to share my story on such a public stage. I feared the judgment I would receive. My agent encouraged me to at least consider meeting her before I said no, and I agreed. During our conversation I was moved by her commitment to mental health and inspired to share my story with her. She told me she was coming to Atlanta and that she would love to have lunch to tell me more about her project. I agreed and met her at the Ritz Carlton for lunch a few days later. I had no idea that our meeting that day would have such a phenomenal impact on my life.

The woman I met with was Jeanne Blake, a medical journalist, author, and affiliated faculty member of the Division on Addictions at Harvard Medical School. She is the creator of *Words Can Work* and president and founder of Blake Works, Inc. Her organizations produce, publish, and distribute evidence-based media to help young people, families and communities talk about the mental health challenges kids face while growing up. I loved how passionate she was about her work, and so after lunch I agreed to do the project. Jeanne was the first to give me a platform on which to share my story. And sharing my story helped me to become stronger and more confident.

When we first started the interview on film I chose my words carefully. As the interview carried on I started to pull the layers back and reveal the real me. The more honest I was, the more powerful I felt. Once the project was complete, I watched that video over and over. When I told my therapist, he agreed that going public really helped me get over my shame and move on with my life.

I was fine not playing in the WNBA. The people with the Atlanta Dream organization would always make little jokes with me about coming to play for them. After one game I was waiting for a friend outside the Dream locker room when head coach Marynell Meadors approached me. She asked how she could get me back in a jersey. I appreciated her words but laughed it off as just being a playful comment. I was enjoying my summer and had no intentions of rejoining the WNBA.

At the summer's end I headed back to Poland to start to prepare for the season. In November during a game I hurt my knee and had to come home to have minor surgery. While I was home rehabbing my knee I got a call from my agent saying that Marynell Meadors wanted to meet with me. I agreed and we met at a café in Midtown Atlanta the following week. Over lunch she asked me if she could get my rights from L.A. I told her that she could, but that I wasn't ready to commit to playing. She told me I didn't have to make a commitment yet, but if I wanted to play to contact her.

I considered the impact I could have if I came back to play. I thought of all the people I could help by sharing my story and showing I was still successful and strong. If I could change the life of one person, then it might be worth it. I picked up the phone sometime in the New Year and told Marynell I was up for the challenge. I could help lead a young expansion team. Something still wasn't right with my knee, but I figured it was just a process and would get better with time.

CHAPTER 21

Welcome Back to the South

I was really excited about the opportunity to play back in the South. A lot of my fan base was there since I played college at Tennessee and in the S.E.C. I had moved to Atlanta in 2007 because I loved the energy of the city. Several friends from college lived in Atlanta, and I felt I would be received well and supported by them. When I was out in L.A the fan support was different from my experiences in DC and at UT. L.A. is a big city and people are awfully busy there. The Sparks were one of the most storied franchises, just behind the Houston Comets, but our stands were often empty when we played. I was eager to get back to my roots and play in front of the people who had supported me my entire career. The only thing I asked in return from my new franchise was that they be honest with me. If I was going to come back and play it was important for me to have an open line of communication. Once they promised that, I was ready to put my name on the dotted line.

My agent faxed me a copy of the contract and I looked it over. It was a standard contract, but he wanted me to make sure certain clauses were included. He made sure we both equally agreed to the things in my contract. The day I signed, my agent wanted me to take the copy of the contract we received with me to make sure the contract they had me sign was the same one. I headed down to their offices on Walton St. to officially become apart of the franchise. I was handed the contract and told they had agreed on everything with my agent, and that it was ready to be signed. I said okay, and told them I wanted to read over the contract before I signed it. I don't think they expected me to pull out the contract out my purse and compare it to the one they laid in front of me. I skimmed and told them I could not sign the contract they had in front of me. It wasn't the same contract that we agreed upon. I told them they should call my agent and stepped out of the room so Marynell and the president could figure things out.

The media was looking at me and with a smile on my face I said the contract wasn't right. A few minutes later I was called back in and they had my agent on the phone. He explained that they were working it out. They had changed the clause that said that my contract was fully guaranteed even if I had a problem with my knee. When I looked at the contract they wanted me to sign it did not state that. Their contract stated that if I were to hurt my surgically repaired knee my salary would not be fully guaranteed. Their error was rectified and after I signed I was officially a part of the Atlanta Dream.

Once I got into my car after doing press I called Jim Tanner, my attorney with the prestigious law firm Williams and Connolly. I told him how I felt really uncomfortable about what had just happened. It seemed as if they purposefully tried to have me sign the wrong contract. He agreed that there was something shady about the transaction but told me not to worry about it. The situation had been resolved and now regardless of whatever injury I may sustain while playing for them, my salary would be fully guaranteed.

After I signed I started getting lots of messages and letters from supporters who were glad to see me coming back to the game. Just before the season started I sat down with Oscar Dixon from the Associated Press and shared my story about why I stepped away from the game. I was straightforward and clear. I no longer wanted to hide the truth about what

I went through and so I spoke candidly about my experience. A few weeks after my first interview, I sat down with *Sports Illustrated* reporter Kelli Anderson to talk about my story in depth. I was able to open up more and talked about my suicide attempt in Los Angeles. I had never planned to tell anyone in the media about this, but something pushed it out of me. When that article came out in *Sports Illustrated* my Facebook page was flooded with support. People thanked me for going public and said how I had inspired them to keep fighting. During the season I had several writers for different papers apologize for bashing me when I left the team. One reporter, who ridiculed me more than others, apologized and confessed that his wife suffered from depression. He told me that there were days that she couldn't get out of bed. I was glad that I had the courage to be honest. If mental health issues weren't so taboo I might have been more open and honest about what I was going through sooner. I decided to make it my mission to save the next person from the embarrassment I'd felt.

My new team was so much fun. The team was comprised of a young group of players who wanted to play together and do well. Each day I came to practice I was inspired by the team's energy and wanted to give them all I could to. I felt my presence was making a positive impact. Unfortunately, during the final stretch of the season I had to bow out and have another surgery on my knee. Another MRI revealed that I had a cartilage deficiency and should not be playing. I was disappointed that I could not continue on with the team and help them through the playoffs. Even though we lost in the first round I was excited about the future of the franchise. I had helped them go from 4-30 to 18-16, and we had created a buzz around the league.

For the first part of the off-season I rehabbed my knee and made it stronger, and in January I headed to Cyprus to test it out. While I was there all I could think about was getting back to the states and helping my team win a WNBA Championship, but meanwhile my team was thinking otherwise. I should have taken it as a sign when I had that situation happen with the contract early on. After we agreed on a buyout I signed with the

San Antonio Silver Stars. The franchise was the most professional team I'd ever played with. All I had to do was my job; there was no pettiness. But it was also the least athletic team I had played on my whole career. We were smart but not very strong, and as a big guard it was my duty to guard the best guards on the other team. That was something I wasn't expecting, but I was optimistic about the potential of this team and wanted to do whatever I could to contribute in an effective way. I enjoyed coming to work every day and really appreciated the positive work environment.

Moving to Texas for the summer was a new experience in and of itself. The heat was suffocating. There were times when I would wake up in the morning to take my dogs for a walk and the temperature was already nearing triple digits. Whenever I had friends come to visit the heat would be the first thing they would mention. We had hot summers in New York, but nothing like this. Life without air conditioning in Texas in the summer is something I wouldn't wish upon my worst enemy.

As the season progressed both of my Achilles became inflamed and made it difficult for me to practice. When I got out of the bed in the morning I moved around my apartment at the pace of a turtle. I would wake up each morning stiff and sore. My aches and pains really had me feeling like an old lady. My trainer and I followed the treatment protocol but nothing helped. I would take anti-inflammatory meds and ice to help with the day-to-day discomfort. As we headed into the All-Star break I agreed to have medicine injected in the bursa of my right Achilles. It was painful, but it almost instantly helped me feel better. After the All-Star break I began to play really well. We were coming together as a team and making a strong push for the playoffs. Our team had great potential and it seemed as if we were finally playing to it. My body was feeling good and I was looking forward to helping my team through the playoffs. It was a few days after my thirty-third birthday when the inevitable happened. In a game against Minnesota, we were on defense and I had just closed out the shooter. I took a step with my right foot and felt someone kicking me. After it happened I fell to the floor and clutched my foot. As they were helping me off the court it felt like there were bricks in my foot. I insisted that a player on the other team must have kicked me. When we looked back at the tapes I saw that no one was around me at the time of my injury. I had in fact just stepped up when my Achilles ruptured. After coming to grips with the probable diagnosis, I returned to the bench in a boot to cheer my team on the rest of the game.

The following day we returned to San Antonio and I had an MRI. After a few hours of waiting the results were in and it was revealed that I had fully ruptured my tendon. In the back of my mind I'd hoped that it was just a bad sprain. At 33 years old this injury could be career ending. I told myself that I would do everything it took to walk away from the game—my first love and the thing that had given me so much strength—on my own two feet.

A few days later I had surgery to repair the damaged tendon. I was disappointed that I was unable to finish out the season with my team, but I was thankful to have a great trainer and teammates there to help me. I couldn't walk, so they made sure I had food in my apartment and that my dog was taken care of. When it came time to return back to Atlanta they packed up my apartment and car for me. This injury was especially difficult for me because it forced me to have to depend on other people. I have always been independent, so for me to have to ask for help was difficult.

Through the process of recovery I have often looked to my mother for inspiration. Her fight to stay sober for 19 years has motivated me to push through the adversity of this injury. I am privileged to have her in my life and I am proud of the strides she has made to be a better mother. We've had many, many bumps in the road but her determination is admirable and I aspire to it. And I also, every day, make sure to thank and remember the woman who gave my mother such strength, which she then passed down to me. The three of us prove that love and faith can be guides through the darkness.

Overtime

I remember when I used to journal as a kid; my grandmother would sneak around and read what I had written. I of course felt violated by her intrusion, but I now know that it was her way of checking on me. I have always been able to express myself better on paper than with words. Before I took on this project, I talked to Tony Gaskins Jr. I wasn't sure where to begin or how to start. He gave me hope and encouraged me to write for at least an hour a day. I did that and more, some days. My words flowed from my head onto the pages and I buried myself in my work like I used to do with basketball. I plunked myself and my sore tendon in front of my computer for hours on end. I was not only healing physically from my injury but also recovering emotionally. As I wrote I saw myself transform.

My purpose became clear and I found myself delivering my testimony to whoever would listen. Jeanne Blake, who was the first to tell my story about depression, asked me to participate on a panel. We partnered with the Satcher Health Leadership Institute of the Morehouse School of Medicine to help spread the message. The forum is designed to increase mental health awareness through a series of town hall-style forums around the country, entitled NFL Community Huddle: Taking a Goal Line Stand for Your Mind & Body. This partnership works to educate, motivate and mobilize communities to work together to address mental health issues like dementia, depression, stress, and drug and alcohol abuse. The forums were led by Dr. David Satcher, who was the 16th U.S Surgeon General under the Clinton Administration and is the head of Satcher Health Leadership Institute. While part of the panel, I had the opportunity to share my stories in major cities with NFL teams. I was received well and that gave me more confidence in my public speaking ability. I was able to see how my story impacted the lives of those I shared it with. Speaking has become a passion of mine and it is extremely rewarding, so much so that I have often contemplated doing it full time.

As I have recovered from this injury I have wanted to call it quits several times and join the business sector. However, when Coach Summitt came forward with her own diagnosis, she gave me strength. When I sat with her at her home the weekend after she went public about her diagnosis of dementia, she assured me that she was going to do all she could to fight her disease. Her mantra throughout her battle has been, "Dementia has never fought against an opponent like Pat Summitt." Like her, I'm the type of person who doesn't mind taking the road less traveled. My story has been my glory.

All that being said, I can't wait to get back out there on the court.

Acknowledgements

F irst of all I would like to thank Tony Gaskins Jr. and Jay Gilmore for helping me birth this book. Without you two guys I would have never gotten the courage to share my story. Special thanks goes to Jennifer, you have been an amazing friend to me. You believed in me when I didn't believe in myself. Thank you for your patience and understanding. I would also like to thank my friends Rita, Monica, Antonio, Adena, Marni, Shana and India. I appreciate you all for letting me run my ideas by you and for being honest about my writing. Lastly, I cannot forget all of my ride or die fans and supporters who have been there through all my ups and downs this story is for you.

the stranger finds no grace in her stride,
no beauty in her smile,
no strength in her aggression.

in his educated mind, no lesson can be found in her story.

her earned muscles,
       too strong.
her clean skin,
       dull.
her inherited stature,
       awkward.

his eyes glance, but see no gleam.
but they needn't see it.

undeterred, she keeps on.
behind her stretches a bumpy road,
cleared with met challenges,
paved with dedication.

ghosts of ancient mold-breakers whisper the way.
with a brave heart and a curious mind, she treads on,
because the instant that his vision informs her path,
we are all lost.

"raw grace"
Laini Madhubuti Lee

15302489R00138

Made in the USA
Lexington, KY
19 May 2012